Quilt As-You-Go
MADE CLEVER

Add Dimension in 9 New Projects

● IDEAS FOR HOME DECOR ●

Jera Brandvig

stash BOOKS®

an imprint of C&T Publishing

Text and photography copyright © 2021 by Jera Brandvig

Photography and artwork copyright © 2021 by C&T Publishing, Inc.

Publisher: Amy Barrett-Daffin

Creative Director: Gailen Runge

Acquisitions Editor: Roxane Cerda

Managing Editor: Liz Aneloski

Editor: Karla Menaugh

Technical Editor: Debbie Rodgers

Cover/Book Designer: April Mostek

Production Coordinator: Tim Manibusan

Production Editor: Alice Mace Nakanishi

Illustrator: Mary E. Flynn

Photo Assistants: Lauren Herberg and Gabriel Martinez

Photography by Jera Brandvig, unless otherwise noted

Published by Stash Books, an imprint of C&T Publishing, Inc., P.O. Box 1456, Lafayette, CA 94549

Library of Congress Cataloging-in-Publication Data

Names: Brandvig, Jera, 1985- author.

Title: Quilt as-you-go made clever : add dimension in 9 new projects : ideas for home decor / Jera Brandvig.

Description: Lafayette, CA : Stash Books, an imprint of C&T Publishing, Inc., [2021]

Identifiers: LCCN 2021012527 | ISBN 9781644030233 (trade paperback) | ISBN 9781644030240 (ebook)

Subjects: LCSH: Patchwork quilts. | Patchwork--Patterns. | House furnishings. | Miniature quilts.

Classification: LCC TT835 .B66338 2021 | DDC 746.46--dc23

LC record available at https://lccn.loc.gov/2021012527

Printed in the USA

10 9 8 7 6 5 4 3

Dedication

Dedicated to my husband, Benjamin Brandvig. Thank you for reminding me to make time for what's important, not only for our family but for myself as well. I feel like anything is possible when we're in it together!

This photo was taken after a long week of virtual school and working from home amidst the lockdown/pandemic. What better way to spruce up our sweatpants and long, fluffy hair than a quilt?

Also, thank you to my boys, Ethan and Simon, for always telling me my "blankets" are beautiful! Your compliments come at the perfect moments when I'm feeling unsure or too tired to keep going. My favorite kind of crafting will always be when I'm making things with the two of you.

Acknowledgments

Thank you so much to my quilty friend Lisa Garber (a.k.a. @TheCurvyQuilter on Instagram) for your excitement and enthusiasm for this book and for contributing your talents to share your beautiful quilts with the world!

Contents

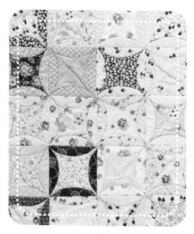

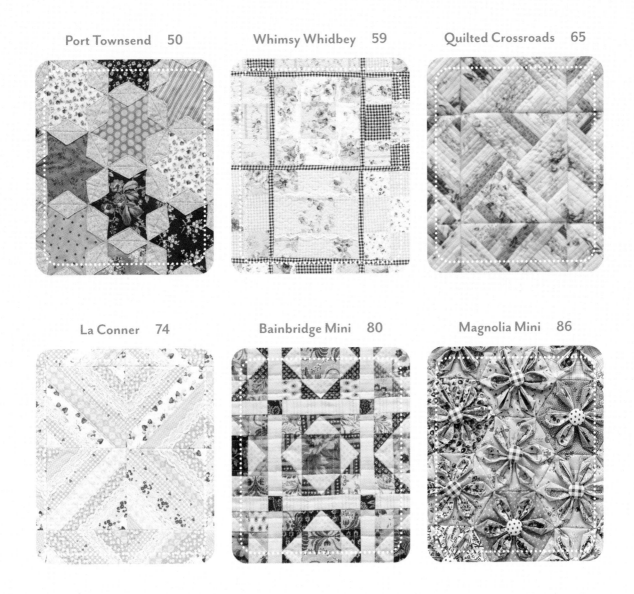

Introduction

HOW IS THIS BOOK DIFFERENT?

If you have followed my creative journey, you may have heard of my first two books, *Quilt As-You-Go Made Modern* and *Quilt As-You-Go Made Vintage* (page 112), in which I teach how to apply the quilt as-you-go (QAYG) technique to both modern and classic-style quilts. My quilty journey continues with this book, where I expand on QAYG by showing completely new ways to use the technique, while adding creative embellishments to your projects such as ribbons, buttons, and lace.

Similar to my other books, my intention for this one is for it to be more than a book of patterns. This book will teach you fresh techniques to expand your quilting repertoire and, most importantly, spark creativity in your inner artist. My hope is that you will be excited to start a project as well as expand on these techniques later on. Think of this book as an anthology of undaunting projects assembled using various techniques, including fabric origami, quilt as-you-go, hand stitching, embellishing with ribbons and lace, as well as traditional quilting.

START SMALL, THEN GO BIG

I've always strived to keep it simple yet creative, and I've stayed true to that. If there's ever a project that seems daunting, we will start small so that you learn the technique, and then you can choose to go bigger when you're ready. Also included are home decor ideas on how to display your quilted minis in your home.

A SHORT MESSAGE FROM JERA

My goal is to spark creativity for you and most importantly to have fun! *While a lot of people see quilting as a hobby of precision and following patterns to a T, I've always tried to look at it from a different angle.* (In *Quilt As-You-Go Made Modern*, you can see the evidence of this in my improvisational quilting methods!) Being creative means taking risks and doing things outside of the norm—if people weren't creative, everything would look the same. If you're a seasoned quilter, I hope this book lets you see quilting from a creative and new perspective. If you're a new quilter, welcome! I hope this book makes quilting not seem so daunting; but most importantly, I hope this book gives you the quilting bug.

Decorating Your Home with Quilts

What made you decide to start quilting? Maybe you learned how to quilt from a loved one or a friend? Maybe you follow a crafter who inspired you on social media? Or perhaps like me, you're obsessed with beautiful fabrics?

It's always been about the fabrics for me, which has come full circle now that I design my own fabric collections. I decided to learn to quilt because I was hoarding fabric. I'd go into my local quilt shop, ogle the fabrics, pick up a fat quarter and charm pack here and there, and display them in my crafting room. My husband thought I was nuts, as I didn't even know how to sew. What better way to display fabrics than a quilt? And so I taught myself and here we are.

I've always seen quilts as an art form, where textiles are my medium and the batting is my canvas. I presented this line of thinking in *Quilt As-You-Go Made Modern*, where I got really creative with improvisational quilting as-you-go.

I love making smaller quilts, not only because you can complete them in a weekend or two, but also because I love to decorate my home with them.

Port Townsend (page 50)

QUILTS FOR THE WALL

Port Townsend (page 50) is the perfect size to hang on your wall behind a console. When I choose fabric for a quilt that I know I'll be displaying in my home as art, I tend to lean toward classic and mature color schemes that are tried and true. My favorite color is red, so I couldn't resist a red and white quilt for this pattern. Traditional blue and white is next on my list.

I wasn't kidding when I said my favorite color is red, as I have an entire red-and-white dish collection! Draping a small quilt on an open cabinet door, whether it be in your living room, dining, or guest room, adds a beautiful pop of color.

Port Townsend
(page 50)

There's a lot to see in this photo! Can you spot *Port Townsend* displayed prettily in my sewing room?

Welcome to my cozy sewing room! It's tiny, but many beautiful quilts and lots of creative inspiration happen right here! That's why it's a must that I surround myself with beautiful projects and pretty fabrics to help keep the creativity flowing.

Port Townsend (page 50) hung on
a small hand-towel rack

Quilt As-You-Go Made Clever

Find a pretty iron towel rack or mini hand-towel rack to easily display your quilts and add beauty to your walls!

TOP: *Sunset Hill* (page 32) draped beautifully on a towel rack in my sewing room

TOP RIGHT: *Kingston* (page 24) looks gorgeous hung in my living room.

BOTTOM RIGHT: Another pretty display idea using Lisa Garber's version of *Sunset Hill* (page 41)

USING BASKETS TO FRAME YOUR QUILTS

I think quilts and beautiful baskets go together quite charmingly. You can use a big basket next to a sofa
to throw your quilts in, or use a small basket to frame a mini quilt to display on your wall.

Three large quilts snuggle beautifully in this large basket.

The first two quilts are from free patterns under the Tutorial tab on my
blog (page 112). On the left is *La Conner Stars* made from my La Conner
collection. The quilt in the middle is *Woodland Rose* made from my
Woodland Rose collection for Lecien Fabrics. On the right is a gorgeous
vintage quilt gifted to me from the Seattle Modern Quilt Guild.

I found this beautiful tobacco basket in the sale bin at my local hobby store. It wasn't in perfect shape, but a quilt fixed that right up! I used little wooden clothespins to hang this mini in the center.

Quilted Crossroads (page 65) and *Sunset Hill* (page 32)

Magnolia Mini (page 86) looks so pretty framed in the center of this round, tobacco-style basket! You can prop it in a corner shelf or hang it on your wall for some added charm!

Magnolia Mini displayed on a corner shelf

TOP: The quilt on the couch is *Madame Fleur*, designed and made by me. The fabrics are from my Madame Fleur collection for Lecien Fabrics. Free pattern on my blog (page 112).

RIGHT: *Magnolia Mini* (page 86) hung on a wall, adds to this cozy corner!

Decorating Your Home with Quilts

DINING ROOM DISPLAY

Sharing how beautiful *Quilted Crossroads* (page 65) can look displayed in a dining room. I have a thing for displaying quilts in there—maybe it's because so much family time is spent in this room, I like to make it as cozy as possible! Some may fear for the quilts (especially mine since I have two boys!), but somehow, they've managed to go unscathed.

Quilted Crossroads (page 65)

A gorgeous red and white vintage quilt that I found at my local antique shop. It wasn't in pristine condition, which made it priced at a bargain and not too scary to hang in my dining room! I made the scrappy table runner for my mom, but it seems to have made its way back to my home. Maybe I "borrowed" it one too many times! I made it from a charm pack by French General for Moda Fabrics.

FRAMING YOUR QUILTS

One of my favorite ways to display a mini quilt is hanging it in an old picture frame or an antique window frame.

My love for blue and white is no secret! But when I had to decide between red-and-white transfer dishes verses blue-and-white, red triumphed, as it is my favorite color. That being said, I had to show a little blue-and-white love in my living room to not hurt any quilt's feelings. *Friday Harbor* (page 42) is mini but mighty! And doesn't it look gorgeous framed in this antique window frame?

Friday Harbor (page 42)

I found this frame at my local crafting store, but you can make your own using an old frame you have on hand. Or search your local antique shop for a vintage frame, as they always have plenty! Just staple twine across the back for hanging your mini quilts. It adds so much charm displayed just about anywhere.

Bainbridge Mini (page 80), displayed atop a console and against a mirror

The vintage colors from *Magnolia Mini* (page 86) inspired me to take out some of my vintage china dish collection, displayed all around the quilt. The wire rack is an organization rack (found at a local hobby store) that I painted white. I knew it would be perfect for displaying my minis!

MORE DISPLAY IDEAS

Here's a charming idea for your smaller quilts! This is a towel rack I found at my local hobby store. Three smallish quilts (up to about 45˝ × 45˝) rolled up fit perfectly!

Towel rack with *Friday Harbor* (page 42) in the center, framed by quilts from *Quilt As-You-Go Made Vintage* (page 112)

If you have room for it, you can't go wrong with a quilt ladder! A ladder displays your quilts beautifully and is so practical, as you can easily pull a quilt from it to snuggle up in. Nowadays you can find so many beautiful vintage-style ladders online or at your local home decor shop.

TOP: Quilt ladder with *Whimsy Whidbey* (page 59) on the left and *La Conner* (page 74) above to the right

RIGHT: Talk about eye candy! The quilt draped on the top left, *Strawberry Shortcake*, is shown in *Quilt As-You-Go Made Vintage* (but its pattern is the quilt named *Red Square*, from *Quilt As-You-Go Made Modern*). The quilt on the top right, *Loyal Heights Red and White Quilt*, as well as the quilt on the bottom, *Loyal Height No-Batting Quilt*, were both made using fabric from my Loyal Heights collection for Lecien Fabrics; free patterns for both are available on my blog (page 112).

Another efficient and practical way to store your quilts is to fold and stack them beautifully on a plant stand. This was foldable plant stand that I found in an antique shop. You'll find that these types of plant stands are inexpensive and a good size for stacking quilts. Plus, it makes for a beautiful display!

Quilts stacked on an antique plant stand

When I first spotted this quilt rack, I thought it would be a unique and charming way to display quilts. Later I learned that its actual purpose is a flower pot stand, but it still works beautifully for quilts!

Madame Fleur draped on an antique flower stand. (For fabric and pattern information about *Madame Fleur*, see the top photo and caption on page 15.)

Photo by Estefany Gonzalez of C&T Publishing

Projects

Being from the rainy city of Seattle, I've always said to "Let your creativity rain!" I hope these projects inspire you to make something, and perhaps look at the quilting craft from a different and fun perspective!

If you're from the Pacific Northwest, you might recognize some of the project titles! I've named all of the quilts after places near and dear to me in Washington.

Happy Quilting-in-the-Rain!

Kingston

FINISHED QUILT: 38″ × 38″ • *Designed and made by Jera Brandvig*

Quilt As-You-Go Made Clever

Near and Dear to Me

Kingston is a little town in the Kitsap Peninsula, a 30-minute ferry ride away from Edmonds (a town north of Seattle). This quilt has a regal look to it, so immediately my mind thought of Kingston, a charming and cozy waterfront town with a main street filled with cafes and an assortment of little shops.

Kingston Ferry

In *Kingston*, I will show you how simple it is to add the beautiful intricacies of ribbon to your projects. The addition of ribbon will turn heads, as it adds that extra something special.

Then, I will walk you through how to finish this using the quilt as-you-go technique so you can complete it all on your own! The QAYG technique makes it easy to quilt intricate designs on each individual block.

This project is great for beginners and a fresh approach for seasoned quilters.

Material Requirements and Cutting

Material			Yardage	What to Cut
Block 1	Dark red mini print	■	⅜ yard	96 squares 1¾˝ × 1¾˝
	Pink small print (I used 2 different pink prints in this quilt.)	☐	¾ yard	96 squares 1¾˝ × 1¾˝ 48 squares 3˝ × 3˝
	Dark red large floral	■	⅛ yard **or** 1 fat quarter	12 squares 3˝ × 3˝
Block 2	Cream print	☐	½ yard	7 squares 8¾˝ × 8¾˝ Bisect each square on both diagonals to yield 4 triangles for each square, 28 triangles total. You will use 26.
	Light pink large floral	☐	½ yard	7 squares 8¾˝ × 8¾˝ Bisect each square on both diagonals to yield 4 triangles for each square, 28 triangles total. You will use 26.
	Dark eggplant ribbon, approx. ⅞˝ wide		8½ yards	*For each block:* 2 strips approx. 11½˝ long Note: Instead of precutting, you can trim ribbon to needed size as you are ready to sew them on.
Batting			⅞ yard (90˝ wide) **or** Prepackaged crib-size (45˝ × 60˝) **or** Batting scraps	*For QAYG technique:* 25 squares approx. 9˝ × 9˝
Backing	Your choice		1¼ yards	No cutting needed.
Binding	Your choice		⅜ yard	4 strips 2½˝ × width of fabric
Other	Coordinating thread for both fabric and ribbon			
	Recommended, but optional: Rotating cutting mat (at least 12˝ × 12˝)			

I used ⅞˝-wide ribbon. Since this is a smaller block, I don't recommend going any wider than 1½˝. The ribbon is by French General for Moda Fabrics.

Photo by Estefany Gonzalez of C&T Publishing

BLOCK ASSEMBLY

Use ¼˝ seam allowances and press seams open.

Blocks 1 and 2 will measure 8˝ × 8˝ trim size,
7½˝ × 7½˝ finished.

Block 1

1. Using the 1¾˝ × 1¾˝ squares, make 4 sets of four-patch units for each block.

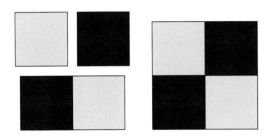

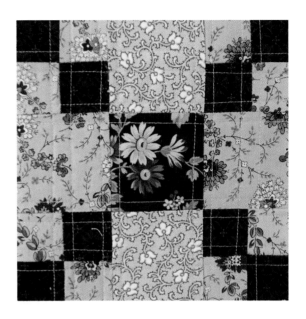

2. Using the units from Step 1 and the 3˝ × 3˝ squares, assemble the block.

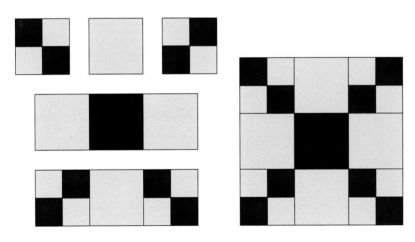

3. Repeat to make 12 blocks.

Block 2

1. Assemble the triangles to complete a block.

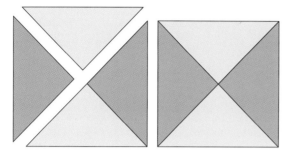

2. Repeat to make 13 blocks.

ADD THE RIBBON AND QUILT AS-YOU-GO!

What's awesome about the quilt as you-go technique is that it's easier to quilt intricate designs since you're quilting one block at a time, as opposed to moving an entire quilt underneath your sewing machine. If you haven't tried this technique before, give it a try! You can do it!

Block 2

1. Center block 2 on a batting square. Flatten with your hand or do a quick press with your iron (try not to touch the iron to the batting). Place a few pins so it doesn't move; you might find later that you can skip the pins.

2. Trim a piece of ribbon so it fits from corner to corner on the diagonal seam of the block. Center the ribbon on the diagonal seam as best as you can, and pin in place.

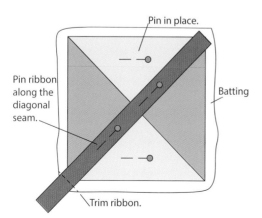

Pin in place.

Pin ribbon along the diagonal seam.

Batting

Trim ribbon.

TIP ● *I usually just eyeball centering the ribbon. When I pin the ribbon in place, I like to place the pins right along the diagonal seam, which helps me visualize if the ribbon is centered. To do this more accurately, you can mark the center of the ribbon at each end. Then align the ribbon centers with the corners of the block, and pin in place along the diagonal seam.*

3. Using matching thread, sew along the edge of the ribbon. Remove pins when they get in the way. This is the first step in quilt as-you-go for this block, since the topstitching to apply the ribbon is stitched right through the batting.

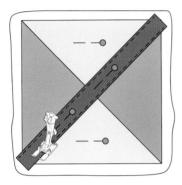

4. Repeat Steps 2 and 3 to apply ribbon on the other diagonal seam. You will sew directly over the first ribbon as you cross over it.

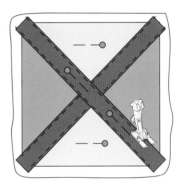

5. Quilt your block! For this block, I quilted simple lines. For evenly spaced lines, align the edge of the sewing foot along the previously stitched line.

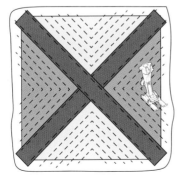

TIPS ●

- *Make sure your quilting stitch starts and ends at the very edge of the fabric block (it's okay to start and end your stitch slightly on the batting to ensure this).*

- *I typically quilt with a 2.0–3.0 stitch length.*

Quilt As-You-Go General Quilting Rules

You don't have to quilt your block the same as mine. Just be sure to do the following.

· Keep your quilting small, since you're working on a small block. For example, if you want to free-motion and quilt loopy-loops, make them small loops. Big loops will bunch up your block.

· Keep your quilting consistent throughout the block. When you quilt, your block will slightly shrink. This is true for any quilt. Therefore, keeping the quilting pattern consistent throughout your block and for each individual block will help them all shrink evenly.

6. Place the quilted block on a cutting mat and align a ruler with the edge of the block. Trim the excess batting using a rotary cutter. Repeat for all 4 sides.

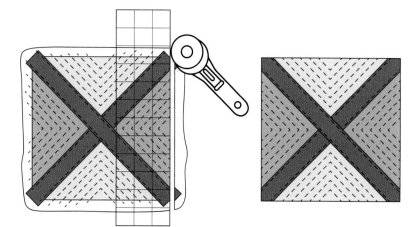

TIP ● *Use a rotating cutting mat to make this part go by super-fast! See My Favorite Tools and Supplies (page 105).*

Block 1

1. Center each block over a piece of batting and smooth it out. Pin in place.

2. Repeat Steps 5 and 6 from block 2 to quilt and trim all 13 blocks. I quilted straight lines along the seams by simply guiding the side of my presser foot alongside the seams.

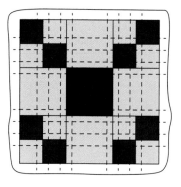
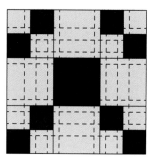

QUILT ASSEMBLY

1. Arrange the blocks in a 5 × 5 formation. Alternate the blocks starting with block 1 in the upper left corner.

2. Sew the blocks together using Method 1: Block-to-Block Assembly (page 95).

Quilt assembly

FINISH THE QUILT

See detailed instructions in Finish It! (page 98).

1. Add the backing fabric, a quick process that requires minimal quilting.

2. Bind your quilt.

Fabrics: A combination of French General and 3 Sisters for Moda Fabrics and Kim Diehl by Henry Glass & Co. Fabrics. The ribbon is by French General. All fabrics were pulled from my beloved fabric stash to make this beautiful combination of colors!

Kingston

Photo by Estefany Gonzalez of C&T Publishing

Sunset Hill

- **PRECUT FRIENDLY:** 10˝ × 10˝ squares
- **FINISHED QUILT:** 39˝ × 39˝

Designed and made by Jera Brandvig

This quilt is assembled using a unique form of quilt as-you-go. It is made up of individual circles that are prepadded with batting. When you sew the circles together to form the quilt top, then stitch down the edges of the circles on the front of the quilt, the stitching creates a beautiful quilted petal design on the back.

Don't let the circles in this quilt intimidate you! It's easier than it looks and is beginner friendly. Simply prepare your circles and then sew them together—and no binding needed!

Near and Dear to Me

This quilt is named after a cozy neighborhood bluff called Sunset Hill in Seattle. Sunset Hill overlooks boats harboring in Shilshole Bay, with picturesque views of the Olympic Mountains in the background. I frequently walk to Sunset Hill with my family to catch the sun setting into the water and rolling mountains.

Front and back of quilt

Fabrics: High Tea collection by Jera Brandvig for Lecien Fabrics (my very first fabric collection!)

Photos by Estefany Gonzalez of C&T Publishing

Material Requirements and Cutting

Material		Yardage	What to Cut
Fabric	Assorted fabric prints (I used 36 fat quarters.)	72 precut 10˝ squares (e.g., 2 precut 10˝ square packs) **or** 36 fat quarters or fat eighths **or** 9 half-yards	*From precut squares:* 72 circles 9˝ in diameter (See Sunset Hill 9˝ Half-circle pattern, page 111, and How to Cut Circles Quickly, next page.) *From fat quarters or fat eighths:* Cut 2 circles from each print, 72 total. (It will be a tight fit for fat eighths, so you might need a few extra pieces of fabric to leave room for cutting errors.) *From half-yards:* Cut 8 circles from each, 72 total.
Batting		1¼ yard (90˝ wide) **or** Prepackaged crib-size (45˝ × 60˝) **or** Batting scraps	36 circles 9˝ in diameter
Other		• Coordinating thread • Fabric marking pen • Circle template: Create your own using card stock and Sunset Hill 9˝ Half-circle pattern (page 111), or just use a 9˝ paper plate.* *Recommended, but optional:* • Rotating cutting mat (at least 12˝ × 12˝) (For details, see Cutting Mats, page 105.) • Card stock or Quilter's Template Plastic gridded sheet (by EZ Quilting): To make a square template	

* I like to keep things simple and inexpensive, so I used a 9˝ paper plate as a cutting guide. You can also check for commercial circle rulers (see My Favorite Tools and Supplies, page 105). There's a tool or notion for just about everything.

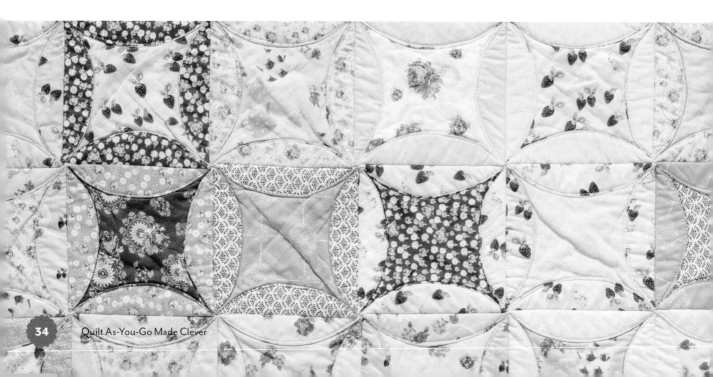

How to Cut Circles Quickly

1. Fold the fabric in half or stack 2 squares to cut 2 layers at a time.

2. I highly recommend using a rotating cutting mat to make this process zip by. Place the fabric on the rotating cutting mat and center a card stock template or a 9″ paper plate on the fabric. Carefully guide the rotary cutter around the template or plate to cut a circle in the fabric. When the positioning starts to get awkward, simply rotate the cutting mat and keep cutting.

3. Use the same process to cut 2 batting circles at a time. I recommend using a 60mm rotary cutter for the batting.

Optional: The Fiskars Fabric Circle Cutter tool, among many others, is a great way to quickly cut circles. To cut a circle, simply fold fabric in half and place the template on top, aligning the folded edge with the bottom marking on the ruler. Position the cutter in one of 11 tracks, depending on the finished circle size you want, press down to expose the blade, and then run it along the track for a smooth cut.

Photo by Estefany Gonzalez of C&T Publishing

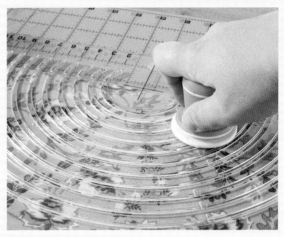

Photo by Lauren Herberg of C&T Publishing

BLOCK ASSEMBLY

Use ¼˝ seam allowances and press seams open.

Prepare the Circles

The first step is making this lovely stack of what I like to call *fabric pancakes*! Because if you're a fabric lover like me, then you'll likely agree they look yummy enough to eat!

1. Start with 2 fabric circles that are different prints. Decide which fabric circle will be the center of the block on the front of the quilt. Cut a small hole 2˝–3˝ long in the fabric circle you decided will be the center/front of the quilt. The hole should be approximately 1˝–1½˝ from the edge of the circle. It will be hidden later when the sides of the circle are folded over.

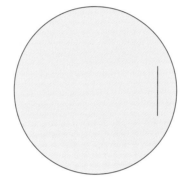

2. Align the circles (one with a hole and one without) right sides together. It doesn't matter which one is on top. Place them on top of a batting circle. Pin or press the 3 layers to help keep in place.

3. Sew all the way around the perimeter of the 3-stack circle, starting and ending with a backstitch.

4. Turn the circles right side out through the hole you previously cut. Run your fingers along the inside edge of the circle to help pop out the curves, then press flat with an iron. The hole will be hidden in the next steps. Make 36 padded circles.

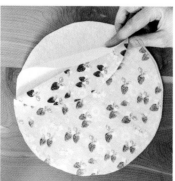

Photo by Estefany Gonzalez of C&T Publishing

Photo by Estefany Gonzalez of C&T Publishing

36
Quilt As-You-Go Made Clever

QUILT ASSEMBLY

Arrange and Mark the Circles

1. Arrange the circles in a 6 × 6 formation. When thinking about where you want your circles to be placed, keep in mind how the back of the quilt will look, as well as what color will be folded over from the back to create the petals in the front.

2. Make a square template to exactly fit inside your circles. Assuming that you sewed a perfect ¼˝ seam allowance around your circles, a 6˝ × 6˝ square should fit perfectly inside the circle with no corners poking out. So, start by cutting a 6˝ × 6˝ square from the gridded plastic template sheet.

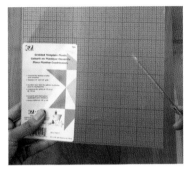

I recommend using gridded plastic template sheet to cut your square template.

Photo by Estefany Gonzalez of C&T Publishing

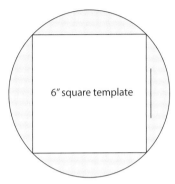

Yay—it fits!

However, if you place the 6˝ × 6˝ square template in the center of your circles and you notice the corners of the template are popping outside the circles, please don't fret! Simply trim off ⅛˝ from 2 adjacent sides of the template to account for any seam-allowance discrepancies.

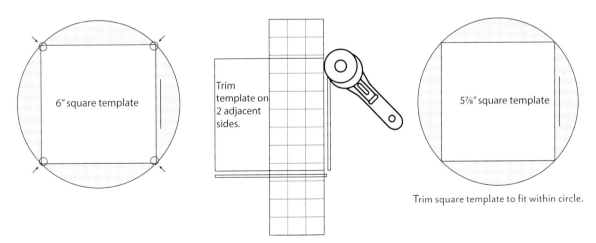

Trim square template to fit within circle.

Note If you trim off ⅛˝ and it still doesn't fit, it's okay to trim off a little more—just be sure the template remains a square. *Also, you need to use the same size of square template to mark all 36 circles. It has to be consistent!*

3. Mark the square template on each circle.

There are three key rules to remember when marking your circles:

- **Mark the side of the circle that has the hole.** These holes will later be hidden when the petals are folded over.

- **Hide your holes!** Make sure these holes will eventually be hidden, so do not put them on the outer edge of your quilt. Also, make sure they're in a spot that will eventually be folded over to form the petals.

- **Mark only the sides where you will be sewing.** In other words, do not mark on the outer edges of your quilt where binding would be if this were a traditional quilt.

Here is an example of how to properly mark a 3 × 3 quilt using the three key rules (at left). The red lines designate where you should mark the lines. Notice

Folded petal hides the hole.

that the outer edges of the quilt are not marked and all holes will eventually be hidden.

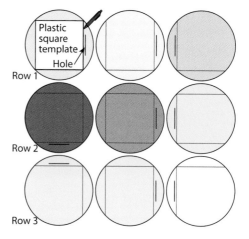

Plastic square template
Hole

Row 1

Row 2

Row 3

After you've laid out and marked all of your circles, it's time to sew!

Sew the Circles Together

TIP ● *Depending on your sewing machine, this process might be easier if you use a walking foot.*

1. Start by sewing the circles within each row together. Place the *backs* (the nonmarked sides) of the first 2 circles together, aligning the marked lines you made using the square template.

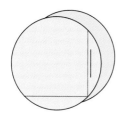

This example shows the first steps of sewing together a 3 × 3 quilt.

TIP ● *Place a pin through both circles along the marked line, then flip it over to see if the pin is aligned with the other marking. This will help ensure everything is lined up.*

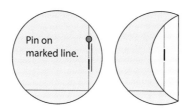

Pin on marked line.

2. When the marked lines are all aligned, sew along the line. Start and end with a backstitch.

3. Add the third circle using the same method.

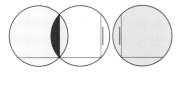

4. Sew the rows together.

Align rows 1 and 2 with *backs* (the nonmarked sides) facing together.

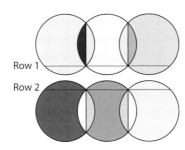

5. Pin at the intersections. Use the pin to make sure the marked lines are aligned on the front and back.

6. Sew along the marked line. *Make sure you sew through both rows at the intersections.* Start and end each stitching line with a backstitch.

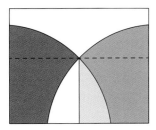

7. Repeat the process to add the remaining rows.

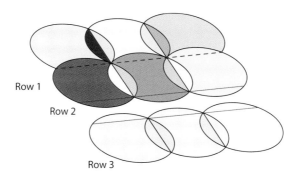

If you make sure to sew through both rows at the intersections, when you open the petals, your intersections will look like this.

Photo by Estefany Gonzalez of C&T Publishing

FINISH WITH QUILTING AS-YOU-GO

Topstitch the Petals

1. Lay the petals down flat by finger pressing or use an iron to press them flat.

2. Use a coordinating thread to stitch them down. I typically use a 2.5–3.5 stitch length, and stitch right along the petal edges. Start and end your stitches with a backstitch.

Sewing along the petals will leave a beautiful quilted pattern on the back of your quilt.

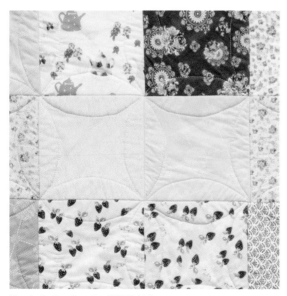

Photo by Estefany Gonzalez of C&T Publishing

No binding needed for this quilt, as the edges are already finished! I did not stitch around the outer edges, though you could if you'd like that finishing touch. Or you could fold over the outer edges and stitch them down to complete each set of petals, making the edges of the quilt straight instead of scalloped.

Optional: Add More Quilting

Feel free to add additional quilting to the center of your circles! Simply add the quilting after you stitch down the petals.

Or you can quilt the circles one-a-time after you have marked the squares but before you assemble them all together. Choose a motif about 3˝ in width and height, to fill a nice space in the center of the block. Choose a simple design that will not change the alignment of your marked squares.

More Project Ideas

For my quilt, I used 36 different prints to showcase the fabrics from my entire High Tea collection—that's a lot! However, you can always simplify the color scheme.

Make All Petals the Same Color

Notice that Lisa used the same gray color for the back of the circles, as opposed to using various colors as I did. The background color is folded to the quilt top to create "petals" that are all gray, giving the quilt a different and more orderly look, yet still stunning! If you choose to make this quilt, be sure to consider if you will use the same backing color for all of the circles, or use various colors.

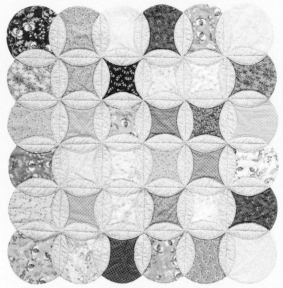

Sunset Hill alternate version, made by Lisa Garber

Fabrics: Madame Fleur collection by Jera Brandvig for Lecien Fabrics (my fifth fabric collection)

Photo by Estefany Gonzalez of C&T Publishing

Make a Three-Color Version

In these three-color variations, the petals will pop if you use the same color for the back of the circles! Simplifying the color scheme is also a fun way to make holiday-themed quilts.

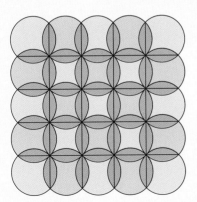

A softer color palette would make a wonderful play mat for a baby gift.

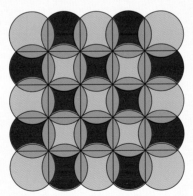

Choose fun holiday prints from reds and greens for a festive wallhanging.

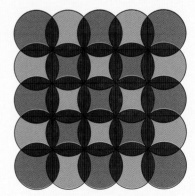

Have fun picking spooky Halloween prints for a quick table topper or wall display!

Friday Harbor

PRECUT FRIENDLY: 2½˝ precut strips • **FINISHED QUILT:** 20¾˝ × 20¾˝

Designed and made by Jera Brandvig

This quilt was made using the quilt as-you-go technique where you piece narrow strips of fabric directly onto the batting. Doing so will give your strips a subtle puffy-quilted appearance, which looks amazing with this Log Cabin–style block!

This is a great beginner project, or perfect if you want to get started on something right away without too much thought and preparation. There's very little preparation because not only do you quilt as-you-go (making for a super quick finish!) but you also cut as-you-go, which allows you to bypass premeasuring all the strips.

If you're feeling overwhelmed with fabric choices, simplify your choices with this two-toned quilt. This quilt is various tones of blue and cream (with a red center for a pop of color). Alternatively, you can grab a jelly roll (a collection of precut 2½˝ strips) and separate the light and dark fabrics into two piles.

Near and Dear to Me

The nautical blues in this mini quilt remind me of the seaside town of Friday Harbor located in the San Juan Islands. What I love about the Pacific Northwest is you're only a ferry ride away from the city, and whichever island you escape to feels like you're far away. Friday Harbor is about an hour drive north of Seattle and a hop onto the Anacortes ferry to the San Juan Islands.

I will always associate this mini quilt with a summertime adventure I took with my boys to Friday Harbor. It's the best feeling when a quilt not only brings beauty, but also fond memories you will forever cherish.

Material Requirements and Cutting

Material			Yardage	What to Cut
Fabric	Assorted blues and cream	☐	½ yard blue and ½ yard cream **or** 4–5 assorted blue and 4–5 assorted cream fat quarters **or** 1 precut 2½˝ strip bundle (Separate light and dark colors into 2 piles.)	From both blue and cream, 10–12 strips 1¼˝ × width of fabric. Put them in 2 piles, ready to be quilted as-you-go. If using precut strip bundle, subcut strips lengthwise to make 1¼˝ × width of fabric.
	Red (center)		Scrap fabric **or** 5˝ × 5˝ square	9 squares 1¼˝ × 1¼˝
	Backing		¾ yard	
	Binding		⅓ yard	3 strips 2½˝ × width of fabric
Batting			⅓ yard **or** Prepackaged craft-size (34˝ × 45˝)	9 squares 8˝ × 8˝

BLOCK ASSEMBLY

Making the Log Cabin Blocks

Use ¼˝ seam allowances and press seams open.

Follow the instructions to make a quilt as-you-go Log Cabin block. I used a cut as-you-go technique (page 46) to make the process go faster.

1. Place a red 1¼˝ × 1¼˝ square in the center of an 8˝ × 8˝ batting square.

2. Trim a 1¼˝ × 1¼˝ square from a cream strip. Align it on the red square, right sides together, and sew, and press open.

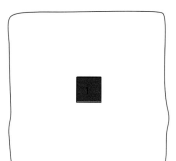
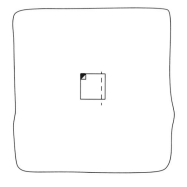
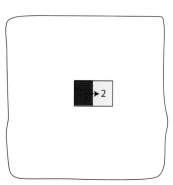

3. Make a cream cut as-you-go a rectangle that's the same length as pieces 1 and 2. Align it, right sides together, sew, and press open.

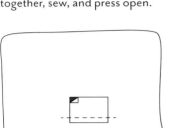

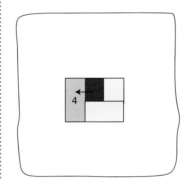

4. Make a blue cut as-you-go rectangle the same length as pieces 1 and 3. Align it, sew, and press open.

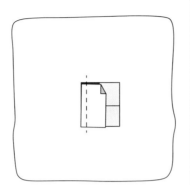

5. Cut a blue cut as-you-go a rectangle that's the same length as pieces 4 and pieces 1 and 2. Align it, sew, and press open.

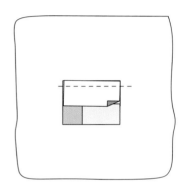

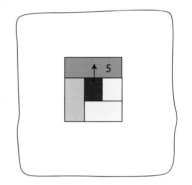

6. Continue adding strips until your block looks like this with 4 logs on each side of the red center square.

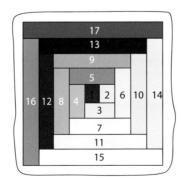

7. Trim the excess batting. Place the quilted block on a cutting mat and align a ruler with the edge of the block. Trim the excess batting using a rotary cutter. Repeat for all 4 sides. To make the process quicker, use a rotating cutting mat (page 105). The blocks should measure approximately 7¼˝ × 7¼˝, depending on how much quilting you added.

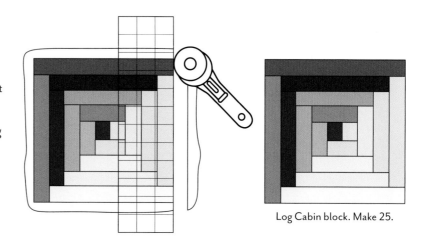

Log Cabin block. Make 25.

Cut As-You-Go

No need to premeasure and precut all the strips before sewing! Instead, align a strip to the length you need it to be. In this example, line it up to the patchwork. Then fold where you need to cut, and use fabric scissors to make the cut along the fold.

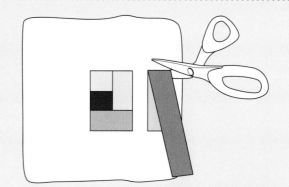

Finger or Roller Press

When the strips are this small, I find it sufficient to finger press the seams flat instead of pressing with an iron. It's Sew Emma makes a fun mini-presser notion that you roll over the seam to press it down (see Quick Press Seam Roller, page 106). Or you can just literally press the seam down with your finger!

Optional: Add More Quilting

Since this block is mini, I opted out of adding additional quilting. However, if you started with wider strips or want to add additional quilting to your mini, you totally can!

Simply quilt lines that are parallel with your seam as you sew on each strip. Remember to keep the amount of quilting consistent to make sure your blocks stay approximately the same size and are not stretched or bunched out of shape.

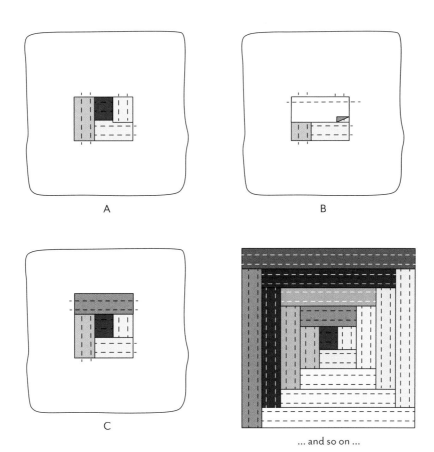

A

B

C

... and so on ...

Or you can choose to add decorative top quilting to each completed block. For this quilt I did not do any additional quilting.

QUILT ASSEMBLY

1. Arrange the blocks in a 3 × 3 formation. For other ways to arrange the blocks, see More Project Ideas (next page).

2. Sew the blocks together using Method 1: Block-to-Block Assembly (page 95).

FINISH THE QUILT

See detailed instructions in Finish It! (page 98).

1. Add the backing fabric, a quick process that requires minimal quilting.

2. Bind your quilt.

Quilt assembly

Friday Harbor

Fabrics: Snowberry by 3 Sisters for Moda Fabrics

Photo by Estefany Gonzalez of C&T Publishing

More Project Ideas

Depending how big you make your quilt, there are so many Log Cabin quilt formations to choose from!
Here are just a few ideas, if you want to make more blocks.

Choose a Different Block Arrangement

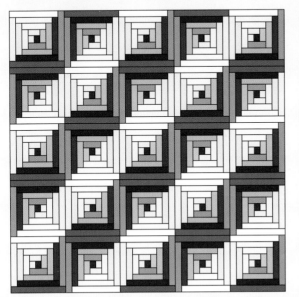 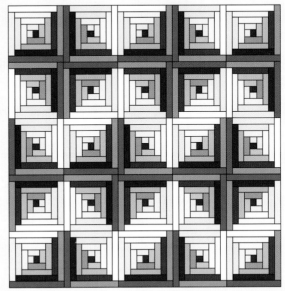

Make an Even Number of Blocks

Use a 4 × 4 formation (16 blocks total), or go bigger using an even number of blocks, for some interesting designs.

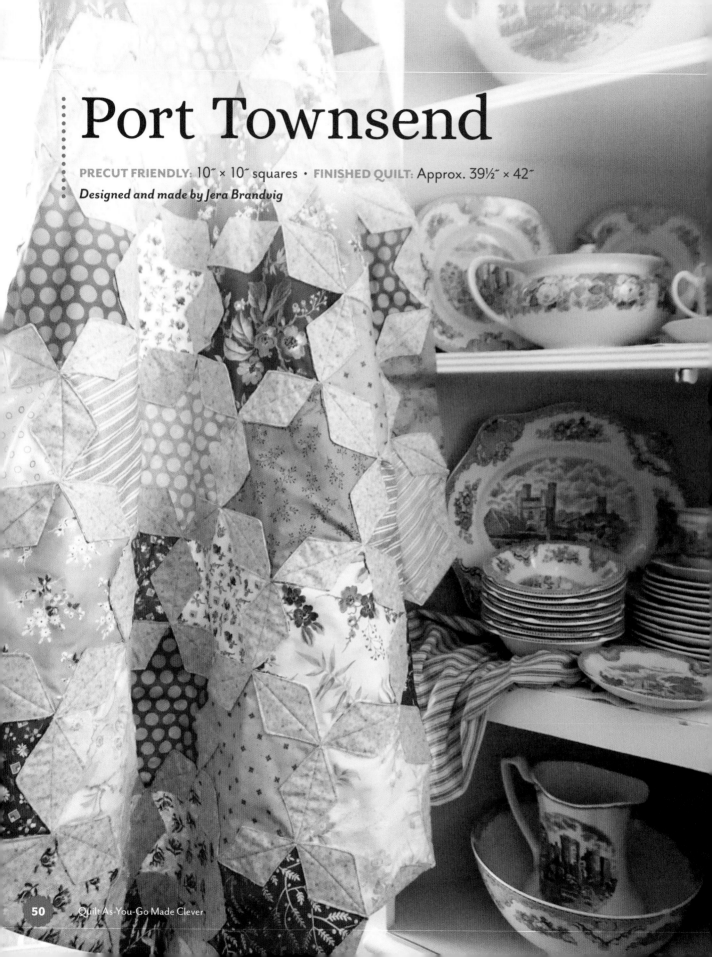

Port Townsend

PRECUT FRIENDLY: 10˝ × 10˝ squares · **FINISHED QUILT:** Approx. 39½˝ × 42˝

Designed and made by Jera Brandvig

This technique is similar to the one for *Sunset Hill* (page 32), but instead of using circles, you start with hexagons. When you sew the hexagons together, stars appear in the middle! This version is a bit lighter than *Sunset Hill*, as it does not use batting. Instead, the backing material is made using cotton flannel for a slightly warmer but still lightweight feel. This makes a perfect lightweight summer blanket or a pretty wallhanging. I used the same beige cotton flannel for all the hexagon backs. The front of the quilt is multicolored, using an assortment of cottons. Using the same color backing fabric, which is later folded and sewn to the front, allows the stars to really pop.

You can always use regular quilting cottons instead of flannel for a super-lightweight quilt, which is perfect to roll up and throw in the stroller. You can also add batting if you wish for a thicker quilt. To see a version made with batting, see More Project Ideas (page 57). Make it bigger for a beautiful coverlet to spruce up the foot of your bed.

Near and Dear to Me

Port Townsend, located in the northwest tip of the Olympic Peninsula in Washington, is a maritime town with a unique history that has left it abundant with Victorian homes and buildings scattered in this small but very charming town. It has brought me lots of inspiration over the years, especially when designing fabric collections. Naming this quilt after Port Townsend resonated with me as I found this pattern to be classic and elegant, yet unique (in the way it is assembled), kindred to this charming town.

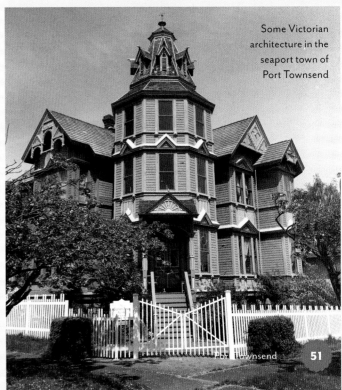

Some Victorian architecture in the seaport town of Port Townsend

Material Requirements and Cutting

Material		Yardage	What to Cut
Fabric	Assorted fabrics for quilt top (stars)	52 precut 10˝ squares (e.g., 2 precut 10˝ square packs) **or** 13 fat quarters **or** 26 fat eighths **or** 11 regular ¼-yard cuts	46 hexagons, measuring 7½˝ from side to side, and 6 half-hexagons (See Port Townsend 7½˝ Hexagon and Half-hexagon patterns, page 110, and How to Cut the Hexagons, Step 2, below.)
	Solid backing material (I used cotton flannel.)	2¾ yards	46 hexagons and 6 half-hexagons (See How to Cut the Hexagons, Step 2, below.)
Other	• Coordinating thread • Fabric marking pen • Card stock or Quilter's Template Plastic gridded sheet (by EZ Quilting): To make a hexagon template		

How to Cut the Hexagons

1. Trace the pattern onto card stock or template plastic and cut it out.

2. Layer your fabric to cut 2 layers at a time. I highly recommend using a rotating cutting mat to make this process zip by. Place the fabric on the rotating cutting mat and center the hexagon template on the fabric.

3. Align the cutting ruler along one side of the hexagon and cut with a rotary cutter. Repeat and cut for all 6 sides, slightly rotating the cutting mat as needed to prevent awkward cutting positions.

As you get comfortable, you can cut 3–4 layers of fabric at the same time for quicker cutting. Cut 46 full hexagon sets and 6 half-hexagon sets.

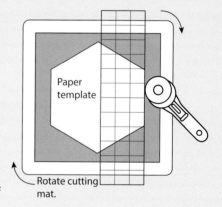

Paper template

Rotate cutting mat.

The first step is making this beautiful stack of 46 hexagons!

BLOCK ASSEMBLY

Use ¼˝ seam allowances and press seams open.

1. Right sides together, pair a hexagon from the assorted colors with a solid backing hexagon. Sew around the perimeter, leaving a 2˝ opening on one side. Start and end the stitching with a backstitch. Clip the corners to lessen bulk.

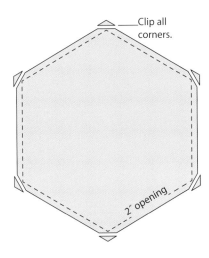

2. Turn right side out. Press flat, and press the seam allowances at the 2˝ opening inward to align with the sewn seams. No need to sew the opening, as you will do this later when you sew the hexagons together.

3. Repeat Steps 1 and 2 to make 46 hexagons and 6 half-hexagons.

QUILT ASSEMBLY

Note the quilt is assembled sideways, so pay attention to the illustrations.

Arrange the hexagons in 7 rows, alternating rows of 7 hexagons with rows of 6 hexagons with a half-hexagon at the beginning and end of rows 2, 4, and 6.

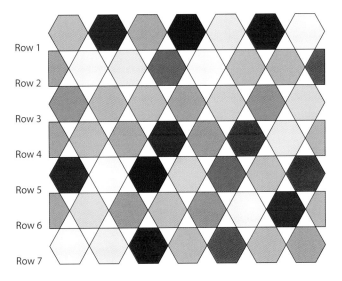

Sew the Hexagons into Rows

1. Mark the center of 2 adjacent sides, and then draw a line to connect the 2 marks. To find the center: Fold one side of the hexagon so that the corners align, as illustrated below. Crease the fold with your fingers, unfold, and then mark that crease with a fabric marking pen. Repeat on the adjacent side so that you've marked 2 centers. Draw a line to connect the 2 marks.

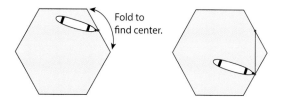

Fold to find center.

2. Align the hexagons with *backs* together, and sew along the marked line. Start and end with a backstitch.

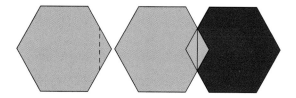

3. Repeat until you've sewn all the hexagons and half-hexagons within each row together.

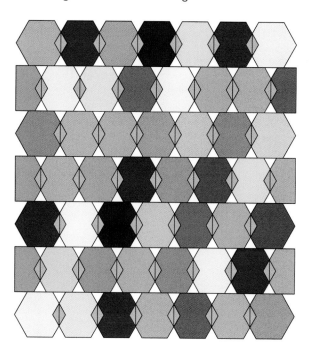

....

Sew the Rows Together

This may seem awkward at first, but I think you will get the hang of it pretty quickly.

1. Mark the center of the sides at the bottom of row 1 and the top of row 2, then draw a line between each set of center marks. This is exactly the way you marked the blocks to be sewn together in a row. Refer to Sew the Hexagons into Rows, Step 1 (above).

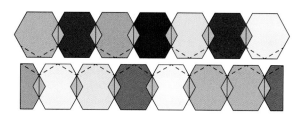

2. Align the back sides of the of the upper corners from row 2 with the back sides of the corners of row 1, as shown by the arrows. Pin as needed to keep in place.

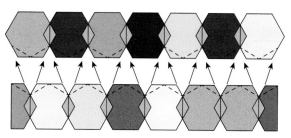

3. Sew along the marked lines. You will be sewing sort of a zigzag line. Pivot at each intersection, taking care to sew through both hexagon layers at the intersections at the ups and downs of the zigzag corners, so that you won't have any gaps in your quilt.

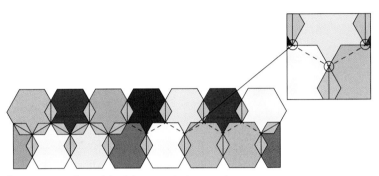

Be sure to sew through both layers at the intersections.

4. Repeat by attaching row 3, then the next row, until all 7 rows have been attached. The image below shows rows 1–6 attached, with all the corner flaps opened up. Row 7 is about to be attached.

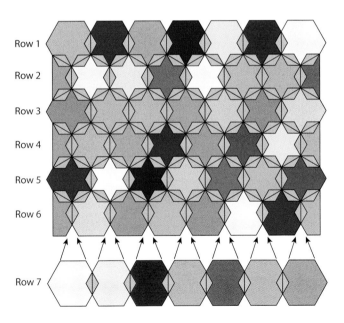

Row 1
Row 2
Row 3
Row 4
Row 5
Row 6
Row 7

Port Townsend

Fabrics: Little Sweethearts collection by Laundry Basket Quilts for Andover Fabrics, Inc.

Photo by Estefany Gonzalez of C&T Publishing

QUILT AS-YOU-GO

1. Fold the flaps down so they lie flat, and you will see a star pattern emerge.

2. With coordinating thread, topstitch the edges of the flaps in place, which also adds a pretty quilted pattern on both sides of the quilt.

3. On the outer edges of the quilt, mark the centers of the remaining hexagon sides and draw a line between the center marks, just as you did in the quilt assembly process. Fold and press the edges flat and topstitch.

Any 2˝ openings from preparing your hexagons from Step 1 will have been stitched closed by now, after all of the top stitching is finished.

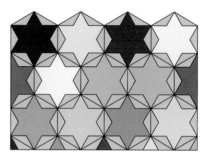

Optional: Add More Quilting

After you stitch down the flaps to form the star shape, don't forget that you can always add additional quilting to the center of your stars. Or in the spirit of quilt as-you-go, you can quilt each hexagon one by one before sewing them together. To do this, use a disappearing-ink fabric pen to mark where the flaps will fold down to form the star, then quilt a small motif in the center of each hexagon.

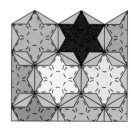

More Project Ideas

Make It with Batting

This alternate version of *Port Townsend* is made from all cotton fabric with batting in the middle, as opposed to the flannel backing that I used for the project quilt. Adding the batting makes for a fluffier and warmer quilt. The padded feel to it could make an excellent play mat for a baby. Or you can go smaller to make a table topper or hot pad for serving warm dishes.

You may notice that this version was finished slightly differently in that there are no half-hexagons. Instead, Lisa trimmed the hexagons ¼″ from the corners. Then she pressed the seams inward and topstitched them down.

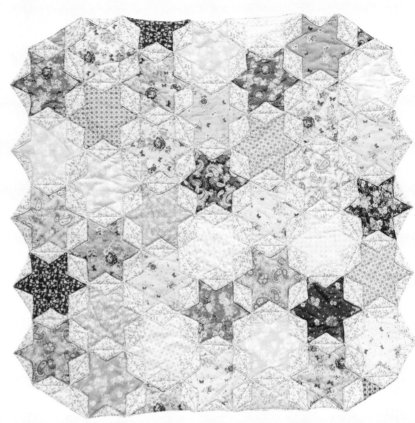

Port Townsend alternate version, made by Lisa Garber

Fabrics: Woodland Rose collection by Jera Brandvig for Lecien Fabrics
(my third fabric collection)

Photo by Estefany Gonzalez of C&T Publishing

This quilt is the perfect way to showcase your favorite fabrics, each framed in a star!

Make a Multicolor Quilt

This mini quilt gives you an idea of how this pattern could look if using various fabrics for the front and back.

Add some batting to this mini and its size would be the perfect table topper.

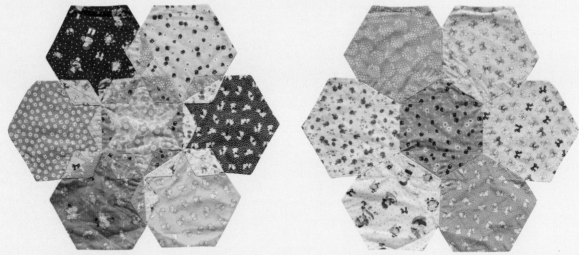

Front of quilt

The back is a beautiful mix of colorful hexagons!

Make Port Townsend Coasters

Instead of connecting the hexagons together to make a quilt or table topper, use a single prepared hexagon to make coasters with stars! These would make quick and unique homemade gifts. Or you can go a little bigger and connect enough hexagons to make a matching table topper or table runner. Add batting for the perfect hot pad or coaster!

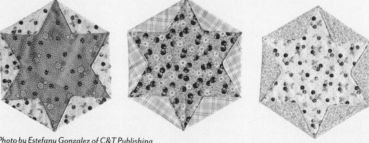

Photo by Estefany Gonzalez of C&T Publishing

Whimsy Whidbey

PRECUT FRIENDLY: 10˝ × 10˝ squares • **FINISHED QUILT:** 43˝ × 51½˝

Designed and made by Jera Brandvig

Near and Dear to Me

Whidbey is one of my favorite places to visit with my family. Located Northwest of Seattle, you can drive there by going through Deception Pass or taking a ferry boat. So while I tapped into my feminine side with the romantic colors and frills when I made *Whimsy Whidbey*, fond memories with my boys on Whidbey Island are at the heart of this quilt.

I love taking a simple idea and freshening it up a bit to make it your own. Adding trims is a fun way to spruce up your projects. Finishing with quilt as-you-go makes it easy (and quick!) to do.

I found crochet lace from my local craft shop, but you also could find a large array of gorgeous vintage trims on eBay or other online sources. Have fun shopping for trims and don't forget that they don't have to match—different lace designs and textures add to the charm.

Though this pattern is very simple and quick to assemble, the added crochet trim makes it stand out. I assembled this quilt using a quilt as-you-go technique where you quilt each individual block and then attach the blocks together using joining strips. I used a red gingham print for the joining strips, which makes the simple blocks pop and really adds to the feminine frill of the fabrics and trims.

When I made this project, I had a little-girl quilt in mind and really tapped into my feminine side with the romantic colors and added frills. Being a mother of two boys where everything seems to do with spiders/bugs, sports, and video games, this project was exciting and breath of fresh air for this mama bear!

Material Requirements and Cutting

Material		Yardage	What to Cut
Fabric	Assorted fabrics for quilt top	30 precut 10˝ squares (e.g., 1 layer cake usually has 42 precut 10˝ squares)	*From precut squares:* 30 squares 10˝ × 10˝
		or 8 cuts ⅜ yard each	*From ⅜-yard cuts:* Cut 4 from each.
		or 15 fat quarters	*From fat quarters:* Cut 2 from each.
	Joining strips	⅜ yard	12 strips 1˝ × width of fabric
	Backing	2½ yards	
	Binding	½ yard	6 strips 2½˝ × width of fabric
Batting		1¼ yards (90˝ wide)	
		or Prepackaged twin-size (72˝ × 90˝)	30 squares 10˝ × 10˝
		or Batting scraps	
Other	Lace trim	16 yards	*For each block:* 2 strips approx. 9˝ long Note: You can wait to cut as you stitch blocks.
	Coordinating thread		

Note I used a quilt as-you-go method where joining strips were used to attach the blocks together. Alternatively, you can use Method 1: Block-to-Block Assembly (page 95) where joining strips are not needed. To give you a third option, you can skip quilt as-you-go and use this pattern but assemble via traditional methods. So many choices!

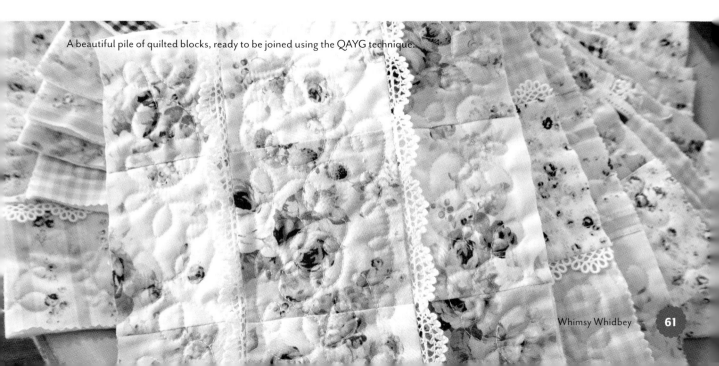

A beautiful pile of quilted blocks, ready to be joined using the QAYG technique.

BLOCK ASSEMBLY

Use ¼˝ seam allowances and press seams open.

Stack, Whack, and Sew

1. Sort the 10˝ × 10˝ squares into 15 coordinating pairs. Stack the 2 squares on top of one another, making sure they align. Press if needed. Put them on your cutting mat (I highly recommend a rotating cutting mat) and make the following "stack and whack" cuts.

2. Cut a 3˝ strip on opposite sides of stacked squares. Do not move the strips.

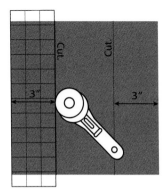

3. Rotate the cutting mat, then cut 3˝ strips on the other 2 sides.

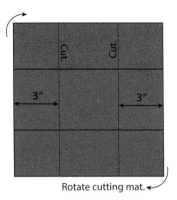

Rotate cutting mat.

After you stack and whack, you will have a total of 18 pieces.

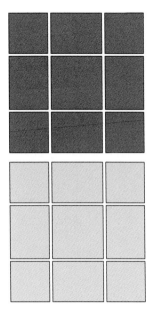

4. Rearrange the pieces, alternating the colors/prints as shown to make 2 different nine-patch units.

5. Sew the pieces in 3 vertical rows, but do not sew the rows together.

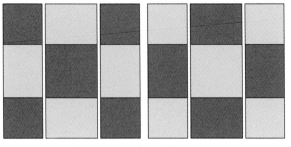

Rearrange as shown, then sew.

Add the Lace/Trim

1. Cut 2 pieces of the lace to the length of your block (about 9˝). Place the lace along the edge of the vertical seamline. With right sides together, attach the vertical rows. This will sew the lace into place. Press the sides of your patchwork open so that the lace is facing outward.

2. Repeat the process for the second block.

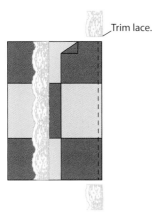
Trim lace.

3. Repeat Steps 1 and 2 to make 30 blocks with lace trim.

QUILT THE INDIVIDUAL BLOCKS AS-YOU-GO

I used the quilt as-you-go technique to finish this quilt. You can choose to use this method or choose to finish it traditionally.

1. Place a patchwork block in the center of a 10˝ × 10˝ batting square. Do a quick press to make sure it's flat. Then, quilt as desired. I free-motion quilted stippling designs and loopy-loops. Just be sure to keep in mind the Quilt As-You-Go General Quilting Rules (page 30). You can start and end your stitches on the batting. Quilt all 30 blocks.

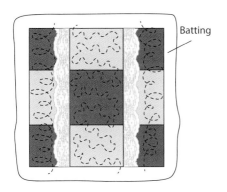
Batting

2. Trim the excess batting off of all 4 sides of the block. I highly recommend a rotating cutting mat to make this process go by quickly. Align a ruler along the edge of the quilt block, then trim off excess batting. Rotate and repeat.

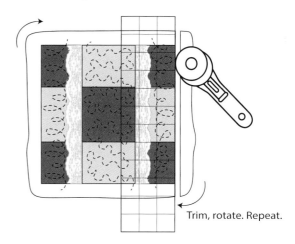
Trim, rotate. Repeat.

QUILT ASSEMBLY

1. Arrange the blocks in a 5 × 6 formation, alternating blocks with dark corners with blocks with light corners. Rotate every other block so the lace strips are vertical on every other block and horizontal on the others.

2. Sew the quilt together using Method 2: Joining Strips on the Front (page 96). Or choose Method 1: Block-to-Block Assembly (page 95) if you don't want the look of ½˝ strips in between your blocks.

FINISH THE QUILT

See detailed instructions in Finish It! (page 98).

1. Add the backing fabric, a quick process that requires minimal quilting.

2. Bind your quilt.

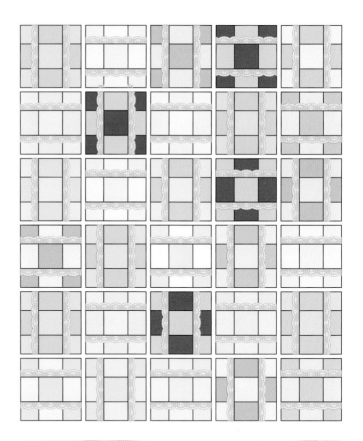

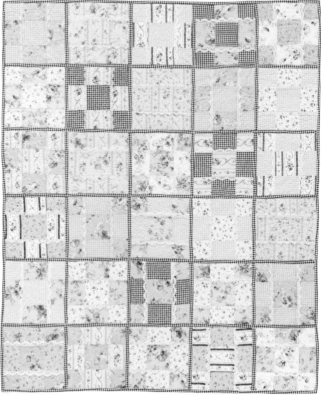

Whimsy Whidbey

Fabrics: Durham Quilt collection for Lecien Fabrics

Photo by Lauren Herberg of C&T Publishing

Quilted Crossroads

PRECUT FRIENDLY: charm pack • **FINISHED MINI QUILT:** 17¾" × 17¾"

Designed and made by Jera Brandvig

Near and Dear to Me

Crossroads is a neighborhood located east of Seattle across Lake Washington. I often take the bridge across Lake Washington so that my boys can visit their grandparents. Furthermore, we have family located all over the country, and even the Philippines. This quilt brings to mind how family is like a quilt. No matter what road we take or where we end up settling, our paths will always be connected, tightly stitched together with warmth, love and memories to be cherished.

This might be one of my favorite patterns in the book. I started by making a small pincushion, then took it a step further with this mini quilt. This pattern looks very intricate, but is actually rather simple because of the quilt as-you-go technique. For a softer look, use scrappy fabrics. But for a more striking look, use two colorways for a three-dimensional look. See More Project Ideas (page 72) for instructions for a pincushion and a pillow, some diagrams for a two-colorway quilt, and ways to make a bigger quilt as well.

Material Requirements and Cutting

Material		Yardage	What to Cut
Fabric	Assorted 5″ × 5″ squares	33 precut 5″ squares (e.g., 1 charm pack usually has 40 precut 5″ squares) **or** Assorted scraps	33 squares 5″ × 5″; subcut each into 1″ × 5″ strips.
	Backing	1 fat quarter	Trim to size of quilt.
Batting		½ yard **or** Prepackaged craft-size (34″ × 45″)	18 squares 6″ × 6″

BLOCK ASSEMBLY

Use ¼˝ seam allowances and press seams open.

Piece and Quilt As-You-Go

1. Piece the assorted 1˝ × 5˝ strips side-by-side onto a 6˝ × 6˝ batting square. You will need to sew 9 strips to cover the entire batting square. This is the first step in quilt as-you-go, since your pieced seams will be sewn directly to the batting.

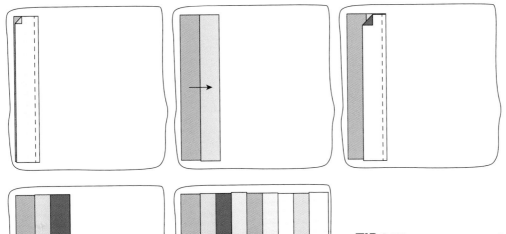

TIP ● *When you sew on a strip, you don't need to press it open with an iron. Instead, just finger press open or use a seam roller (see* Quick Press Seam Roller, *page 106).*

2. Quilt the center of the strips. I quilted simple straight lines right down the middle of each strip. I think the straight lines work well for this block since it's smaller.

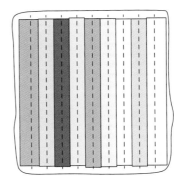

However, the choice is yours! You can quilt diagonal or wavy lines or choose not to quilt the strips at all—whatever looks good to you. Just be sure to keep in mind the Quilt As-You-Go General Quilting Rules (page 30).

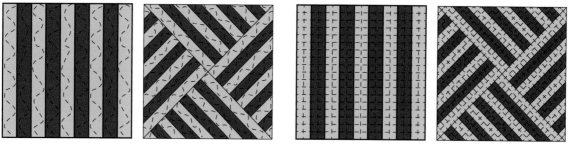

Wavy lines quilted vertically   Straight lines quilted vertically and horizontally

3. Trim the excess batting around the edges so that the strippy square measures 5˝ × 5˝. If you have a 5˝ × 5˝ ruler, you can use that to quickly square up your block. I recommend using a rotating cutting mat to make the trimming go quickly.

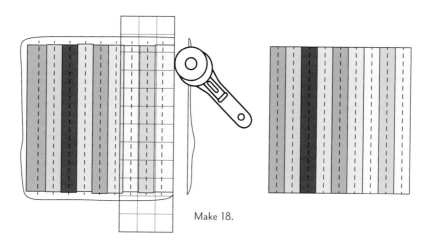

Make 18.

4. Repeat to make 18 quilted strippy squares.

Cut and Reassemble

This quilt is made up of 2 blocks (blocks A and B) that are alternated in the quilt layout. These blocks look almost identical. However, there's a subtle difference in the way the lines are situated and it all has to do with how you cut them.

To make the mini quilt, you will need 9 blocks (5 of block A and 4 of block B), each measuring 6¼˝ × 6¼˝ unfinished.

BLOCK A

1. Place 2 strippy squares on the cutting mat with the strips in a *vertical* position. On each, cut a diagonal line from the top left corner to the bottom right corner. This will yield 4 triangles.

TIP ● *For this particular project, it is very important to clip the corners at a long angle (as shown). This will help prevent bulky seams at the intersections when you assemble the blocks later.*

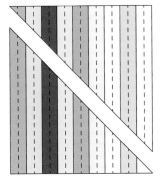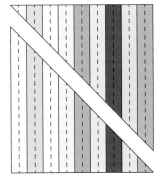

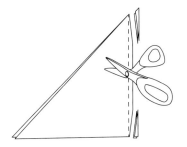

Make sure the strips are vertical before cutting.

2. Arrange the triangles (as shown) to make block A. When you sew the pieces together, don't forget to clip the corners and press the seams open as described in Quilt As-You-Go Assembly Techniques (page 94).

3. Repeat Steps 1 and 2 to make 5 of block A.

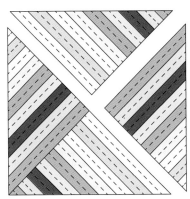

Block A. Make 5.

BLOCK B

1. Place 2 strippy squares on the cutting mat with the strips in a *horizontal* position. On each, cut a diagonal line from the top left corner to the bottom right corner. This will yield 4 triangles.

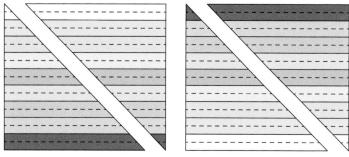

Make sure the strips are horizontal before cutting.

2. Arrange the triangles as shown to make block B. When you sew the pieces together, don't forget to clip the corners and press the seams open.

3. Repeat Steps 1 and 2 to make 4 of block B.

Block B. Make 4.

QUILT ASSEMBLY

1. Arrange blocks A and B in a 3 × 3 formation, alternating blocks starting with block A in the upper left corner.

2. Sew the blocks together using Method 1: Block-to-Block Assembly (page 95).

The back will look like this with all of the seams pressed open. Note that I have clipped each corner seam at a long angle to minimize bulk at the seam intersections.

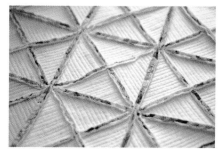

Back of assembled quilt

If you clip the corners of the seam intersections, the quilt won't be bulky from the front.

Quilt assembly

FINISH THE QUILT

See detailed instructions in Finish It! (page 98).

1. Add the backing fabric, a quick process that requires minimal quilting.

2. Bind your quilt.

Quilted Crossroads

Fabrics: Oasis by 3 Sisters for Moda Fabrics

Photo by Estefany Gonzalez of C&T Publishing

More Project Ideas

Make a Pillow Instead

If you'd rather turn this quilt top into a pillow, you will need to make an envelope closure for the backing. You will need a ½ yard of backing fabric and a 17˝ × 17˝ pillow form.

1. From the backing fabric, cut 2 rectangles 17¾˝ × 12˝.

2. On each rectangle, create a hem on the 17¾˝ edge by folding under ¼˝ and press flat with an iron. Repeat with another ¼˝ fold so that no raw edges are exposed. Topstitch along the fold to keep the hem in place.

3. Right sides together, pin the backing rectangles to the pillow front, aligning the raw edges and overlapping the finished edges at the center. Sew all the way around the perimeter.

4. Clip the corners and turn inside out.

5. Optional: If you would prefer the look of a binding edge around your pillow, then sew the backing rectangles to the back of the pillow top but this time with *wrong sides together* in Step 3. Then, add a binding (see Bind Your Quilt, page 100) to cover the exposed raw edges.

6. Insert the pillow form through the envelope opening.

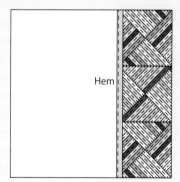

Hem

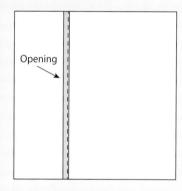

Opening

Make a Bigger Quilt

Make more blocks: If you're loving this block and would rather make a bigger quilt, you can make 56 blocks (28 of block A and 28 of block B), and assemble for a lap-size quilt measuring about 41˝ × 47˝. You'll need about 6 charm packs.

If you want to go even bigger, simply add more blocks. Each block measures 5¾˝ × 5¾˝ finished, so you can use that measurement to calculate how big you want your quilt to be and how many blocks you need to make. You can make about 11 blocks with one charm pack.

… or …

Make bigger squares: In this pattern, 2 squares 5˝ × 5˝ are cut diagonally and then sewn together to create a block that measures 6¼˝ × 6¼˝ unfinished. If you want a larger block, simply start with larger squares. For example, if you start with 2 strippy squares 8˝ × 8˝, you will have a block that measures approximately 10˝ × 10˝ unfinished.

Make a Two-Color Quilt

Try making this quilt in a two-color scheme for a strikingly different look. The contrast of using only two colors gives it more of a three-dimensional appearance.

Block A

Block B

Two-color quilt assembly

Make a Quilt As-You-Go Pincushion

Start small with a pincushion!

1. Sew 1˝ strips onto a 5˝ × 5˝ batting square. Trim so it measures 4˝ × 4˝. Make 2 strippy squares.

2. Cut a diagonal line on each per block A or block B (it doesn't matter which, as long as the strips on both blocks are arranged the same way while you make the cut). This will yield 4 triangles, smaller than the triangles in your mini quilt blocks.

3. Assemble the 4 triangles to make a small block that will be the top of your pincushion.

4. Cut a 5˝ × 5˝ backing square, the same size as your block. Place the pieced block and the backing square right sides together and sew around the perimeter, leaving a small opening on one side. Turn right side out, press, and fill the opening with rice. Stitch the opening closed either by hand or with your sewing machine.

5. Embellish by sewing a button through the center of the pincushion. I made my own fabric button using a button-maker kit (see Add a Cute Button, page 90), which you can find in the sewing section of most craft stores (they usually cost no more than four dollars).

Quilt As-You-Go Pincushion, 4˝ × 4˝, by Jera Brandvig

Fabrics: My La Conner collection by Jera Brandvig for Lecien Fabrics (my second fabric collection)

La Conner

PRECUT FRIENDLY: 2½˝ strips · **FINISHED QUILT:** 36½˝ × 45½˝

Designed and made by Jera Brandvig

A fresh look to this timeless pattern!

A version of this quilt was in *Quilt As-You-Go Made Modern* (page 112). However, this version has more of a romantic look with the addition of lace and softer fabric colors. I use 2½˝-wide strips, making it jelly-roll friendly. I simply start with a big pile of strips and trim them to the length I need using fabric scissors. Remember that you can always use varying widths of strips or even use up your fabric scraps for a completely different look.

Near and Dear to Me

Ever since I was a little girl, it's been an annual tradition to escape the city of Seattle and drive one hour north to La Conner, Washington. While La Conner is known for its breathtakingly endless fields of flowers, my fond memories are drawn from the charming town that is also home to a historic quilt museum and the local U-pick strawberry farms in the valley.

The historic Pacific Northwest Quilt & Fiber Arts Museum in La Conner, Washington, with three of my quilts from *Quilt As-You-Go Made Vintage* (page 112) displayed on the fence!

La Conner, my second fabric collection, was inspired by the town itself! This quilt uses La Conner fabrics and lace.

Material Requirements and Cutting

Material		Yardage	What to Cut
Fabric	Assorted fabrics, jelly-roll friendly	At least 40 precut 2½˝ strips (e.g., 1 precut 2½˝ strip bundle) **or** 12 fat quarters **or** 3 yards of coordinating fabrics in ¼-yard or ⅓-yard pieces	*From fat quarters:* Cut 2½˝ strips along 22˝ length. *From yardage:* Cut 40 strips 2½˝ × width of fabric.
	Backing	2¼ yards **or** ¾ yard (if 90˝–108˝ wide)	
	Binding	½ yard	5 strips 2½˝ × width of fabric
Batting		1 yard **or** Prepackaged twin-size (72˝ × 90˝)	20 squares 10½˝ × 10½˝
Other	Crochet lace (My lace was about 1½˝ wide.)	15 yards	*For each block:* 18˝ long Note: Instead of precutting, you can trim lace to needed size as you are ready to sew them on.

BLOCK ASSEMBLY

Use ¼˝ seam allowances and press seams open.

1. Cut and place a fabric strip exactly along the diagonal that runs from corner to corner on the 10½˝ × 10½˝ batting square. To place the strip accurately, mark the center at each end of the strip and align the centers with opposite corners of the batting square. Pin in place.

TIP ● *To quickly mark the center at each end of the strip, simply fold the strip lengthwise, and crease the fold with your fingertips at each end.*

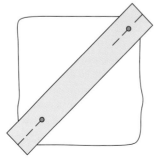

Place the 2½˝ strip exactly centered along the diagonal of batting.

2. Align a second strip along one edge of the center strip. Trim the strip to length using the Cut As-You-Go technique (page 46). Stitch, then press open.

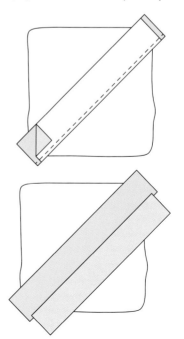

3. Keep adding strips until the batting is covered.

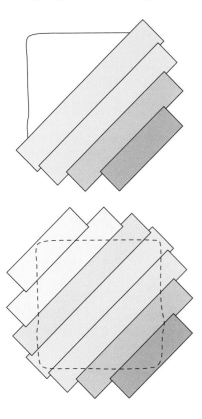

TIP ● *When I added strips, I chose them at random. But remember that you can alternate colors and repeat them, or have all the center strips be the same color, if you really want the diamonds to pop in the quilt.*

4. Square up the block.

- Place the block facedown and trim the excess fabric around the batting. Then, turn the trimmed block right side up.

- Use a 9½˝ × 9½˝ square ruler or template. If you use a plastic template, make sure you mark a 45° line going from corner to corner. Place the square ruler on top of the block so that the 45° diagonal marking is parallel to and as centered as possible with the initial center strip. Maneuver the square ruler around to ensure all sides are within the block while keeping the diagonal marking on the ruler centered within the diagonal strip on the block.

- Trim all excess fabric outside the ruler or template. I highly recommend using a rotating cutting mat for this part so you can cut, rotate, and repeat. This allows for quicker cutting and helps to avoid cutting at awkward angles.

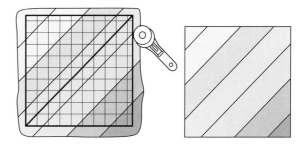

5. Repeat the process to make 20 blocks.

ADD LACE AND QUILT AS-YOU-GO

1. Add 2 strips of crochet lace to each block, placing each an equal distance from the corner of the block. To do this, align the center length of the lace with a seam on your block. Stitch down the center of the lace, right along the seam, using coordinating thread. Trim off excess lace even with the edge of the block.

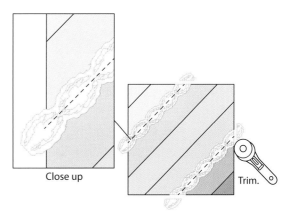

Close up

Trim.

2. Add quilting to your block. I quilted simple straight lines parallel to the seams.

However, don't forget that you can get creative with your quilting! Since you're quilting on a 9½˝ × 9½˝ square as opposed to entire quilt top, free-motion quilting just got a lot easier! Just be sure to keep in mind the Quilt As-You-Go General Quilting Rules (page 30). If your sewing machine has embroidery stitch options, you also could showcase lots of fun stitches on these blocks!

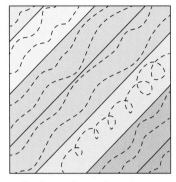

Quilt wavy lines or loopy loops.

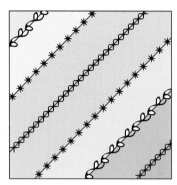

Quilt fun embroidery stitch options from your sewing machine.

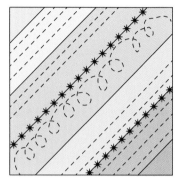

Mix it up with straight-line quilting, free-motion quilting, and embroidery stitches!

QUILT ASSEMBLY

1. Arrange the blocks in a 4 × 5 formation. I alternated the orientation of the blocks so that diamonds appeared.

2. Sew the blocks together using Method 1: Block-to-Block Assembly (page 95).

FINISH THE QUILT

See detailed instructions in Finish It! (page 98).

1. Add the backing fabric, a quick process that requires minimal quilting.

2. Bind your quilt.

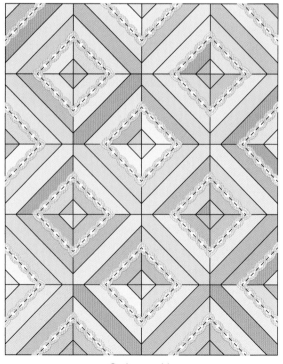

Quilt assembly

La Conner · Fabrics and lace: La Conner collection by Jera Brandvig for Lecien Fabrics (my second fabric collection)

Photo by Lauren Herberg of C&T Publishing

Another Project Idea

Use Colored Lace

Here is another variation of this quilt, made with soft and feminine colors. This was assembled in a 5 × 6 block formation. I love how the La Conner pink lace makes such a pretty frame around the diamonds.

La Conner alternate version, designed by Jera Brandvig, made and quilted by Lisa Garber

Fabrics: Rose Garden collection by Gerri Robinson of Planted Seed Designs for Penny Rose Fabrics of Riley Blake Designs

Photo by Estefany Gonzalez of C&T Publishing

Bainbridge Mini

PRECUT FRIENDLY: charm pack • **FINISHED QUILT:** 14˝ × 14˝

Designed and made by Jera Brandvig

Near and Dear to Me

This project is dear to my heart as I made it on my first weekend sewing retreat with my crafty friends, some of which I taught to quilt many moons ago. We stayed at a little cottage on Bainbridge Island, a 30-minute ferry ride away from Seattle, Washington. We packed our sewing machines and crafted the weekend away. Since then, we have made it an annual crafting getaway staying at different seaside towns where we craft and explore and eat good food to our heart's content. What more could a gal want?

We discovered Molly Ward Gardens in Poulsbo, Washington one evening. It's a restaurant in an old barn surrounded by flowers and antiques with a garden out back—a very magical place!

Sewing machines revved up and ready to sew at our annual crafting retreat.

Mini quilts are such a satisfying project and are great for decorating your home. I love framing mine in an empty picture frame for a little vignette. Use holiday-themed prints to easily customize your decor for the holidays!

In More Project Ideas (page 84), I've also provided instructions to make this into a 15″ × 15″ pillow cover. Or if you love this pattern and want to go bigger, I've provided instructions for that as well.

Material Requirements and Cutting

	Material	Yardage	What to Cut
Fabric	Assorted fabrics for blocks	42 precut 5″ squares (e.g., 1 charm pack) **or** Assorted scraps	For each block, cut: *From light square:* 4 rectangles 1½″ × 2½″ for Flying Geese centers *From dark print:* 8 squares 1½″ × 1½″ for Flying Geese corners *From medium print:* 4 squares 1½″ × 1½″ for corner squares *From second medium print:* 1 square 2½″ × 2½″ for block center
	Cream print	1 fat quarter for sashing	Cut 3 strips 1¼″ × 22″. From each strip, subcut 3 rectangles 1¼″ × 4½″ for sashing; 12 total.
	Red print	5″ × 5″ square for cornerstones	Cut 4 squares 1¼″ × 1¼″.
	Backing	1 fat quarter	
	Binding	1 fat quarter	4 strips 2½″ × width of fat quarter

BLOCK ASSEMBLY

Use ¼″ seam allowances and press seams open.

1. Make 4 Flying Geese units using the 4 light 1½″ × 2½″ rectangles and the 8 dark 1½″ × 1½″ squares.

- Start by marking a diagonal line from corner to corner on the back of each square.

- Right sides together, align a square on one end of the rectangle. Sew directly on the marked line. Trim the remaining fabric ¼″ from the seam. Press open.

- Place a square on the opposite end of the rectangle and repeat the process to complete a Flying Geese unit.

2. Using 4 Flying Geese units, 4 medium 1½″ × 1½″ squares, and the medium 2½″ × 2½″ square, assemble the block. It will measure 4½″ × 4½″ unfinished.

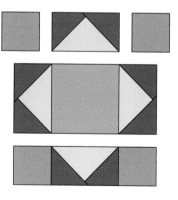

3. Repeat Steps 1 and 2 to make 9 blocks.

QUILT ASSEMBLY

1. Arrange the blocks in a 3 × 3 formation, with sashing strips and cornerstones between the blocks.

2. Sew the pieces in each row together. You will have 3 rows of blocks with vertical sashing strips and 2 rows of horizontal sashing strips with cornerstones.

3. Sew the rows together to complete the top.

FINISH THE QUILT

I did not use any quilt as-you-go finishing techniques for this mini, as it's almost as small as a block! I stitched straight lines parallel to the seamlines for a classic look that didn't take too much attention away from the fabrics.

Baste the backing, batting, and quilt top together and quilt as desired. Bind to finish it (page 98).

Quilt assembly

Bainbridge Mini

Fabrics: Atelier De France collection by French General for Moda Fabrics

Photo by Estefany Gonzalez of C&T Publishing

More Project Ideas

Make a Pillow Instead

You will need a 15˝ × 15˝ pillow insert and 2 fat quarters for the backing.

1. From the sashing fabric, cut 4 additional 1¼˝ strips. Trim 2 strips to 1¼˝ × 14˝ and 2 strips 1¼˝ × 15½˝ for the borders.

2. Attach the 1¼˝ × 14˝ borders to the top and bottom of the pieced top. Attach the longer borders to the sides.

3. Add batting and quilt the top.

4. Cut 2 backing rectangles 12˝ × 15½˝ to make an envelope closure so that you can insert a pillow. To attach the envelope closure, see the detailed instructions for *Quilted Crossroads*, Make a Pillow Instead (page 72). *Optional:* Add a binding to finish.

Make a Bigger Quilt

If you love this timeless pattern and want to make a bigger quilt, you can make this 61½˝ × 71˝ quilt (lap-size). If you want to go bigger, then simply add more blocks. Keep in mind that a charm pack (42 precut 5˝ × 5˝ squares) can make about 10 blocks with good variety.

To make this bigger quilt, make 195 blocks. Assemble as shown in the mini, except in a 13 × 15 formation.

To use precuts, you will need 20 charm packs or 5 packs of precut 10˝ × 10˝ squares. Or you can use yardage, as indicated in the chart below.

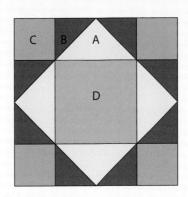

Material		Yardage	What to cut
Fabric	Fabric A (light print)	2¼ yards	780 rectangles 1½˝ × 2½˝
	Fabric B (dark print)	2¾ yards	1,560 squares 1½˝ × 1½˝
	Fabric C (medium print)	1½ yards	780 squares 1½˝ × 1½˝
	Fabric D (medium print)	1 yard	195 squares 2½˝ × 2½˝
	Sashing	1¾ yards	Cut 46 strips 1¼˝ × width of fabric; subcut 362 rectangles 1¼˝ × 4½˝.
	Cornerstones	¼ yard	168 squares 1¼˝ × 1¼˝
	Backing	4 yards	
	Binding	⅝ yard	8 strips 2½˝ × width of fabric
Batting		2 yards (90˝ wide) **or** Prepackaged twin-size (72˝ × 90˝)	

Magnolia Mini

MINI QUILT SIZE: Approx. 18˝ × 20˝ • *Designed and made by Jera Brandvig*

Photo by Estefany Gonzalez of C&T Publishing

Near and Dear to Me

Magnolia is a neighborhood in Seattle that sits on a peninsula in the Puget Sound. I have fond memories taking my kids to the rocky beach front overlooking the West Point Lighthouse at Discovery Park. As this project unfolds you will see it bloom into the namesake flower that this beautiful area is named after.

This darling three-dimensional piece of wall art is easier than it looks. See More Project Ideas (page 92) to assemble the hexagons in varying formations to make an even smaller mini wall art piece, a table topper for a buffet or side table, or an ornament to hang or for gifts.

Material Requirements and Cutting

Material		Yardage	What to Cut
Fabric	Assorted fabrics for front and back of hexagons	11 fat quarters	*From each fat quarter:* 3 or 4 hexagons, 38 total (See Port Townsend 7½˝ Hexagon pattern, page 110, and How to Cut the Hexagons, page 52.)
Other	19 button embellishments (For details, see Add a Cute Button, page 90.)		
	• Coordinating thread and needle		
	• Card stock or Quilter's Template Plastic gridded sheet (by EZ Quilting): To make a hexagon template		

BLOCK ASSEMBLY

Use ¼˝ seam allowances and press seams open.

Prepare the Hexagons

1. Right sides together, pair 2 hexagons and sew around the perimeter, leaving a 1˝ opening on one side. Start and end the stitching with a backstitch.

2. Clip the corners to lessen bulk, then turn right side out. Press flat, and press the seams from the opening inward to align with the sewn in seams.

3. Close the opening. I closed mine by stitching it closed using coordinating thread on my sewing machine. Be sure to prepare your hexagons *without* batting.

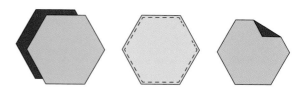

Gather the Corners

1. Find the center of your hexagon by folding it in half, and then in half again. Pinch the folded corner with your fingers and then unfold. There will be a crease in the center of the hexagon from where you pressed the corner with your fingers.

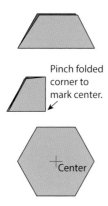

Pinch folded corner to mark center.

Center

2. Thread a needle with about 40˝ of thread, pulling the needle to the center with the thread ends even. No need to tie a knot. Poke the threaded needle up through the center of the hexagon, leaving 5˝–6˝ tails on the back. Make a stitch through each corner of the hexagon, from front to back.

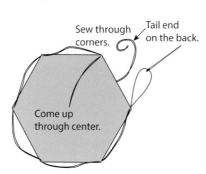

Sew through corners.
Tail end on the back.
Come up through center.

3. After you've sewn through all the corners, take the needle back down through the center of the hexagon to meet with the 5˝–6˝ tail you left on the back (from Step 2). Remove the needle but be sure to leave about 5˝–6˝ at each tail end of the thread. Pull the tail ends together. The corners will start to gather toward the center, forming your soon-to-be petals.

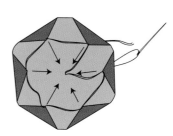

4. When the thread has been pulled tight and the corners gathered in the center, tie the tail ends of the thread in a double knot at the back center of the hexagon. Trim excess thread.

Form the Petals

This is the magical part! After you've gathered the corners, you'll notice 6 little flaps of fabric. These will become the petals.

1. First, push one of the flaps down as shown.

2. Pinch the edge and pull it up toward the corner of the hexagon so that the inside fabric of the petal is exposed.

3. Stitch the petal down as shown by the X in the illustration. To quickly stitch my petal down, I adjusted my sewing machine to a small stitch length (size 1.0–2.0) and used coordinating thread to sew a forward stitch and a backstitch a couple times to make sure it was secured. You may hand stitch if you prefer.

Stitch.

4. Repeat for all 6 petals.

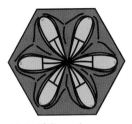

Make 19 flower hexagons.

Add a Cute Button

The finishing touch is to add a cute button embellishment in the center of your flower. I made my own fabric buttons using an easy fabric button kit by Dritz, which has all the tools you need, including easy-to-follow instructions, to make custom fabric buttons.

Fabric button kit by Dritz. You can find these at your local craft / sewing shop.

Photo by Estefany Gonzalez of C&T Publishing

To attach the button, thread it through the center as shown and tie a double knot at the back of the flower hexagon.

QUILT ASSEMBLY

If you've ever done English paper piecing, then simply use your favorite hand-stitching method to sew the hexagons together as you would via EPP.

Quilt assembly

I hand-stitched my blocks together in rows, then sewed the rows together. Here are some tips.

• Join the hexagons right sides together. Using coordinating thread, thread a needle and tie a double knot at the tail end.

• Use a ladder stitch / slip stitch or an invisible feather stitch (see Invisible Hand Stitches, next page) to sew the hexagons together.

How to Start and End a Knot

Before you begin stitching, start with an anchor knot at the corner of one hexagon as shown in the illustration. What you're basically doing is sewing a loop, and then tying a knot through it. You can repeat this at least 2 times. When you sew this knot, you only need to nick the edge of the fabric. You will use this same technique to end your stitch when you run out of thread and need to tie it off.

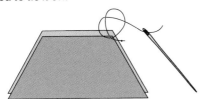

Invisible Hand Stitches

Here are a couple easy hand-stitching guides to sew your hexagons together. Always sew with right sides together, and don't forget to start and end with a knot.

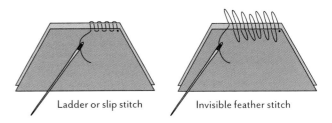

Ladder or slip stitch   Invisible feather stitch

Magnolia Mini • Fabrics: Assortment from my fabric stash, including the collections Retro 30's Child Smile and Flower Bouquet by Lecien Fabrics; Mary Rose by Quilt Gate; Pam Kitty Picnic by Pam Kitty of LakeHouse Dry Goods; and Rosewater by Verna Mosquera for FreeSpirit Fabrics

Photo by Estefany Gonzalez of C&T Publishing

More Project Ideas

Make an Even-Smaller Mini Quilt

This would make a cute mini wall decoration hung in the center of a shabby chic frame! You will need a total of 7 finished flower hexagons. To do this, cut a total of 14 fabric hexagons (7 for the back and 7 for the front).

Make a Table Topper

This would make a darling table topper for a side table or buffet. You will need to make a total of 16 finished flower hexagons. Cut a total of 32 fabric hexagons (16 for the back and 16 for the front). This finishes at about 11″ × 24″.

Magnolia Mini smaller alternate version,
11″ × 11″, made by Jera Brandvig

Fabrics: Antique Rose collection by Lecien Fabrics

Photo by Estefany Gonzalez of C&T Publishing

Make an Ornament

Make a single flower hexagon for pretty ornaments or gifts during the holidays! Use festive fabrics and secure a ribbon with a loopy-loop at the top.

Magnolia Mini ornaments,
approx. 4½″ × 4″, by Jera Brandvig

Photo by Estefany Gonzalez of C&T Publishing

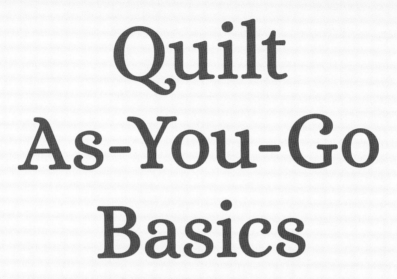

Quilt As-You-Go Basics

In this section, you'll find an overview of two of my quilt as-you-go techniques and how to finish your quilt. Some information may sound familiar if you've read my first two books.

You'll also find some of my favorite quilting supplies and tools. Having the right tools makes the projects so much easier!

Quilt As-You-Go
Assembly Techniques

You're ready to move on to this chapter if you can say yes to these two things:

• Have you quilted your blocks directly onto batting squares?

• Have you trimmed the excess batting (or excess fabric, depending on the project) from your blocks?

Then you are ready to assemble your prequilted blocks using the quilt as-you-go technique!

If you're familiar with my first two books, then you've seen these two QAYG joining techniques. I am providing these techniques in this chapter so you can have them at your fingertips:

• Method 1: Block-to-Block Assembly

• Method 2: Joining Strips on the Front

Note I have a third QAYG method with joining strips on the front and back. That technique was not used in this book, but you can find it in *Quilt As-You-Go Made Vintage* (page 112).

After you've joined your blocks using either method, the last steps are to use minimal quilting to add backing, then to bind your quilt as shown in Finish It! (page 98).

METHOD 1: BLOCK-TO-BLOCK ASSEMBLY

Use ¼˝ seam allowances and press seams open.

This is a subtle way to join your blocks without anyone ever realizing it was quilt as-you-go! If you don't want your blocks to be framed with strips, then use this joining technique.

TIP ● *Depending on your sewing machine, it might be easier to use an even-feed walking foot instead of your regular sewing foot when sewing your blocks together. This foot will prevent the layer of batting and fabric from puckering or shifting around.*

In this method, you assemble the quilted blocks the same way you would assemble the blocks of a traditional quilt, but with the following two exceptions:

- *Always backstitch at the beginning and end of each seam* to prevent the seams from coming open during assembly.

- *Press seams open and trim at the corners.* Use a steam setting to quickly press the seams open. Try not to iron the batting. You can also press the seams on the front of the quilt as well. To prevent bulky seams on the quilt top, trim all the corners of the seam allowances at a long angle.

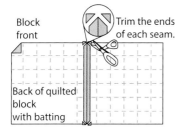

1. Sew the blocks within each row together. Press seams open and trim corners.

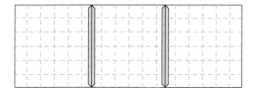

2. Sew the rows together. Place pins at each intersection to keep the rows from shifting. Press seams open and trim the corners at long angles.

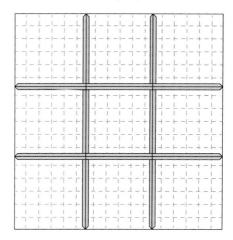

3. *Optional:* Press the seams on the front of the quilt.

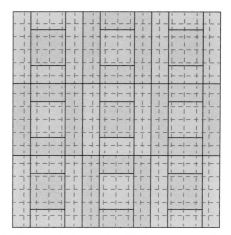

The front will look smooth, with all seams nice and flat.

To finish your quilt, refer to Finish It! (page 98).

METHOD 2: JOINING STRIPS ON THE FRONT

Use ¼˝ seam allowances and press seams open.

With this method, a ½˝ finished strip connects the blocks on the front of the quilt only. The look will be similar to a sashing strip. This method is a great way to subtly frame your blocks or break up a busy pattern.

The joining strips have no batting when they are sewn to the blocks, so you do not have to press seams open or trim corners. After a strip is sewn to a block, press the seam allowances toward the joining strip, which will back it with batting from your block.

1. Cut strips 1˝ × width of fabric. Trim a strip to the length of the block.

2. Place a joining strip on top of the block, right sides together, and align the edge of the strip with the side of the block. Stitch together, starting and ending with a backstitch.

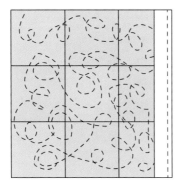

Whimsy Whidbey (page 59) blocks sewn together using joining strips

3. Press the joining strip toward the seam allowance.

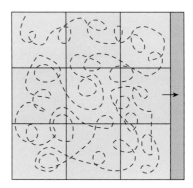

4. Align another block along the opposite edge of the joining strip, right sides together, and stitch.

Stitch.

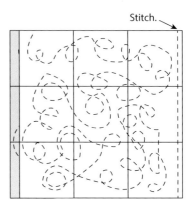

5. Flip the block open, right sides facing up, and press the seam allowances toward the joining strip.

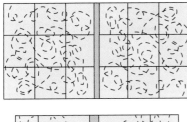

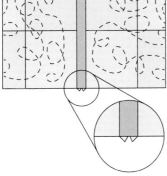

Make sure the seam allowance is pressed toward the joining strip. The joining strip will measure ½˝ finished.

The joining strip will be backed with batting from the two seam allowances.

6. Repeat the process to stitch the blocks in each row together.

7. Assemble the rows together by cutting longer joining strips the same length as the row of blocks. You may have to sew some strips together to make the strips long enough. Then, repeat the process to stitch the rows together using the longer joining strips. *Place pins at the intersections to make sure your blocks line up.*

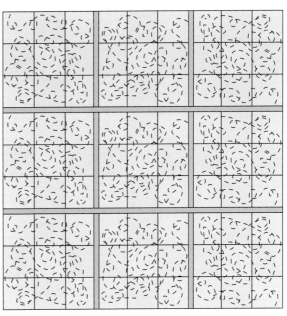

Front of a quilt with joining strips

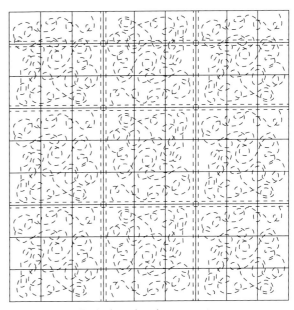

Back of a quilt with joining strips

Finish It!

ADD THE BACKING FABRIC

If you used quilt as-you-go joining Methods 1 or 2 (page 94) to assemble your quilt, then all you need to do is add the backing fabric and bind it. *Minimal quilting is needed to add the backing fabric.*

Here are some examples showing the backs of quilt as-you-go projects, to help you visualize the small amount of quilting needed to attach the backing.

I assembled *La Conner* (page 74) with Method 1: Block-to-Block Assembly (page 95). To attach the backing, I stitched in-the-ditch at the seams to form a grid.

I used joining strips on the front of *Whimsey Whidbey* (page 59). To attach the backing, I quilted a top stitch along each side of the joining strips.

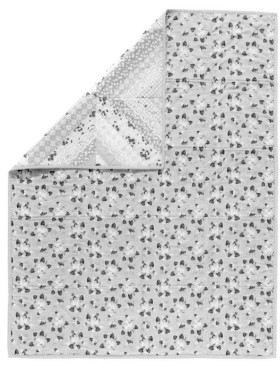

Back of *La Conner* (page 74)

Photo by Lauren Herberg of C&T Publishing

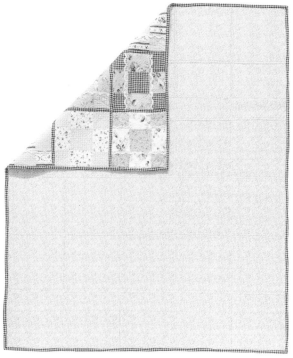

Back of *Whimsy Whidbey* (page 59)

Photo by Lauren Herberg of C&T Publishing

Why Use Quilt As-You-Go If You Still Need to Attach Backing?

With a traditional quilt, you would need to use hundreds of pins to baste all three layers (quilt top, batting, and backing) to keep them from shifting while you quilt designs on your quilt top. This can be challenging, especially if you have to bunch a large quilt underneath a small sewing machine.

However, if you use the quilt as-you-go technique, all your blocks will already have been quilted onto the batting individually and then assembled. You need to baste only two layers together, requiring far fewer pins. And, since all of the intricate quilting is complete, you will need to add only minimal quilting to attach the backing fabric.

Baste

The first step is to baste your quilted quilt top to the backing fabric.

TIPS ●

- *Try using cotton flannel for the backing. Flannel naturally adheres to the batting on the back of your quilt top! Plus it makes for a super-cozy and warm backing material.*

- *I recommend using curved safety pins. The curve of the pin pops back up into the quilt for quicker pinning.*

- *Painter's tape works great for holding down the backing fabric.*

1. Start by placing the backing fabric, wrong side up, on a hard-surfaced floor or on a quilt wall if you have one. Smooth it down as much as possible and tape down all 4 corners. If your quilt is big, I recommend taping down the sides as well. The goal is to make sure the backing fabric doesn't shift around when you place the quilt top over it.

2. Center the assembled quilt on top of the backing fabric, right side up. Smooth the top flat and pin it to the backing fabric. Place pins at each seam intersection and at the end of each seam.

In the following example, X marks the places to put pins.

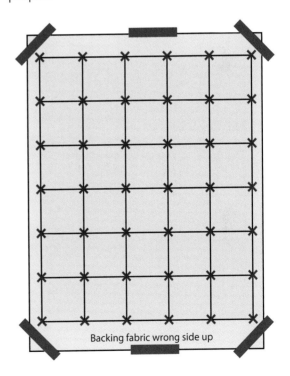

Backing fabric wrong side up

After you've competed pin basting, you can remove the painter's tape and stitch the quilt together.

You need to baste only 2 layers (your prequilted top and the backing), so minimal pins are needed. Yay!

ATTACH THE BACKING FABRIC USING MINIMAL QUILTING

Depending on your machine, I recommend using an even-feed walking foot for this part.

Since all of your quilting is finished, you need to add only minimal and subtle quilting to attach the backing fabric. You can choose to quilt just the horizontal seamlines, vertical seamlines, or even zigzags. Or you can quilt every seam as I did to form a grid.

Once you've decided how you want to attach the backing, either stitch in-the-ditch or quilt alongside the seams. Remove the basting pins as you quilt.

Stitch in-the-Ditch

Stitching in-the-ditch is sewing directly into the seam-line so that you can't see the stitches on the front of the quilt.

Quilt Lines Parallel to the Seams

Quilting lines parallel to the seam work well for quilts with joining strips between blocks, or if you want to add additional quilting to your quilt top.

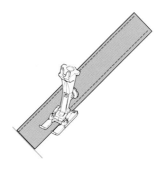

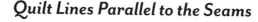

BIND YOUR QUILT

To bind your quilt, prepare the binding strips and sew them onto the perimeter of your quilt. Finish the binding with a blind stitch by hand or a machine stitch.

Prepare Binding Strips

1. Start by cutting 2½˝-wide strips across the width of fabric.

TIP ● *To calculate how many binding strips you need to cut and how much yardage you need, add 10˝ to the total perimeter of your quilt top. Divide that number by 40˝ (the width of fabric) to see how many strips you will have to cut. Multiply that by 2½˝ to calculate the yardage.*

Example: *If the total perimeter of the quilt top is 220˝, you will need 230˝ divided by 40˝ = 5.75 binding strips. Round this up to 6 binding strips. Since each binding strip is 2½˝ wide, you will need 6 × 2½˝ = 15˝ of fabric, which can be rounded up to ½ yard.*

2. Sew the strips together with diagonal seams to create one long binding strip. To sew a diagonal seam, align 2 strips right sides together so that they are perpendicular to one another. Sew a diagonal line from the top left corner to the bottom right corner. Trim the seam allowance to ¼˝ and press the seam open.

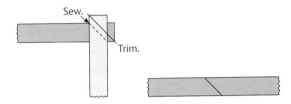

3. Press the binding in half lengthwise so that the width measures 1¼˝.

4. Unfold one end of the binding strip and fold one corner over as shown. Press. Refold the binding strip in half lengthwise.

Photos by Diane Pedersen of C&T Publishing

Attach the Binding

Use a ¼˝ seam allowance to bind your quilt.

TIP ● *If you plan to blind stitch the binding to the back of the quilt by hand, then machine stitch the binding to the front of the quilt. I think blind stitching looks the best, though it does take some extra time.*

If you plan to machine stitch both sides of the binding, start by attaching the binding to the back of the quilt. With this option, you will be able to see a stitching line parallel to the binding on the back of your quilt.

1. Starting with the diagonally folded end of the binding strip, pin the binding on a side of the quilt, away from all corners, aligning the raw edges of the binding with the quilt edge.

Open the binding and sew 4˝–5˝.

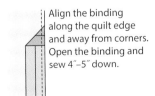

Align the binding along the quilt edge and away from corners. Open the binding and sew 4˝–5˝ down.

2. Refold the binding. Start sewing the binding onto the quilt approximately 3˝ from the folded end, overlapping the previous stitching by at least 1˝. This will create a 3˝ open "pocket" at the beginning of the binding.

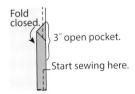

Fold closed.

3˝ open pocket.

Start sewing here.

3. Stop stitching ¼˝ away from each corner and backstitch 1˝. Lift the presser foot and needle. Rotate the quilt one-quarter turn.

End stitching ¼˝ from corner.

Fold the binding at a right angle so it extends straight above the quilt and the fold forms a 45° angle in the corner.

Then bring the binding strip down even with the edge of the quilt. Begin sewing at the folded edge.

4. When you get to the end, you will come upon the pocket that you created in Steps 1 and 2. Tuck the unfinished end into the pocket and continue sewing until you cross over your beginning stitches.

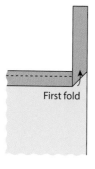

First fold

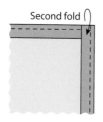

Second fold

Repeat for the remaining 3 corners.

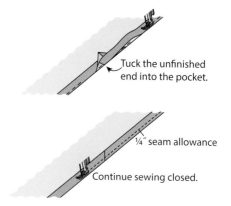

Tuck the unfinished end into the pocket.

¼″ seam allowance

Continue sewing closed.

Finish the Binding

Fold the binding over the raw edges of the quilt back and pin. When you get to the corners, fold the bottom edge of the binding straight up and then pin the corners down to keep everything in place.

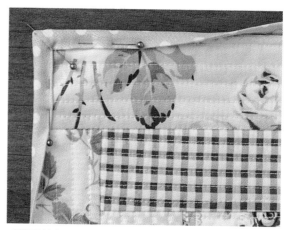

Photos by Diane Pedersen of C&T Publishing

To finish the binding, you can either blind stitch it to the back of the quilt, or machine stitch it to the front.

BLIND STITCH

This may seem like it will take forever. But once you get the hang of it, it goes by more quickly than you would think.

1. Thread a needle with about 3 feet of thread. Don't go any longer, or you'll get knots as you are blind stitching. Start by hiding a knot underneath the binding. Use the knot diagram below to create a starting knot. You can repeat this a couple times to make sure it is sturdy.

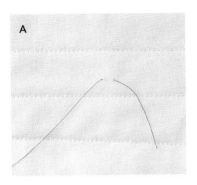 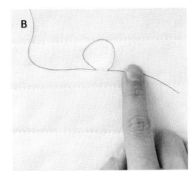 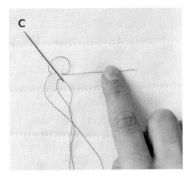

Knot diagram: *(Fig. A & B)* With your needle and thread, make a loop. Hold the thread's tail so it does not slip out. Then *(Fig. C)* put the needle through the loop to create a knot. Repeat a couple of times.

Photos by Diane Pedersen of C&T Publishing

2. To blindstitch, push the needle through just a few threads in the binding edge and then straight down into the quilt. Bring the needle up approximately ¼˝ away from where you started. Repeat.

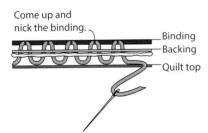

Come up and nick the binding.
Binding
Backing
Quilt top

3. When you get to a corner, stitch through the corner fold to fasten it. When you near the end of the thread, tie it off with another knot.

MACHINE STITCH

To finish the binding by machine, topstitch the binding in place from the front. Machine binding will create a top stitch on the front side of the binding and a line of stitches parallel to the binding on the back of the quilt.

1. Align the edge of the binding with the middle of your walking foot and adjust the *needle width* so that it is 1–2mm from the edge of the binding.

Photo by Diane Pedersen of C&T Publishing

2. Stitch, guiding the edge of the binding strip along the center of the walking foot.

3. Slow down as you approach the corners. Remove the corner pin and replace it with the sewing machine's needle. With the needle still down, lift the walking foot and pivot the quilt 90°. Put the walking foot down and continue sewing.

My Favorite Tools and Supplies

Cutting Mats

• **24˝ × 36˝ and/or 18˝ × 24˝ cutting mat** (by Fiskars)

Use this for cutting fabric and batting. I've recommended Fiskars rotating cutting mats since my very first book as they are good quality and affordable.

• **14˝ × 14˝ rotating cutting mat**

If you've read my other two books, you'll know that this is a quilting essential! This mat rotates 360°, which makes squaring up blocks and cutting circles, as mentioned in *Sunset Hill* (page 32) faster as it prevents awkward cutting positions. It is one of the tools that I use the most.

Rotary Cutter

• **60mm rotary cutter**

This is my go-to rotary cutter and size—it's perfect for cutting through batting and through layers of fabric!

Cutting Rulers

• **3˝ × 18˝ and/or 6˝ × 24˝ ruler** (by Fiskars)

Use these longer rulers to cut batting and fabric. I admit that I love Fiskars rulers because they come in pink!

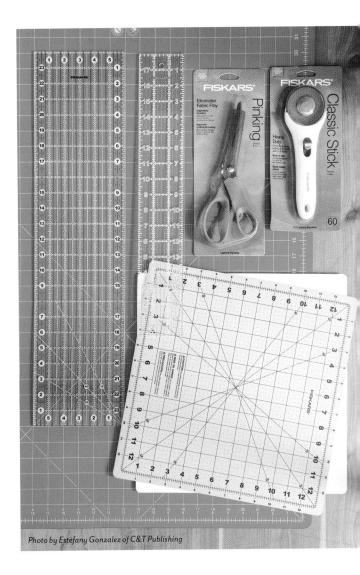

Photo by Estefany Gonzalez of C&T Publishing

Even-Feed Walking Foot

Every sewing machine is different, and you may find that you don't need this. However, if you're having trouble sewing through thick layers of fabric and batting, or if you're getting lots of puckering in your fabric, an even-feed walking foot might be a good solution. You can find universal even-feed walking feet online or at your local sewing machine store, or look at your sewing machine brand's website.

Every sewing machine has feed dogs that pull the fabric from the bottom—they're like little teeth that come out from the machine and help pull what you're sewing along. An even-feed walking foot adds teeth to the top as well. With feed dogs on the top and bottom of the fabric, the layers of the quilt feed evenly through the machine, preventing any puckering. It can also help to sew through thick layers of fabric and batting.

Fabric Scissors

I use these for cutting batting as well as trimming joining strips and cutting the corners off of the seams. For details, see Quilt As-You-Go Assembly Techniques (page 94).

Other Sewing Essentials

- **Cute pincushion** with sturdy pins. (See the adorable pincushion made by Lisa Garber, using fabrics from my La Conner collection for Lecien Fabrics.)

- **Wonder Clips** (by Clover) are a great pinning alternative for certain projects!

- **Stainless steel embroidery snips** are great for hand sewing. (These snips are part of my Woodland Rose fabric collection.)

- **Cotton thread.** I've always been a fan of 100% cotton thread by Connecting Threads. It's affordable, amazing quality, and comes in beautiful colors! It's sturdy and won't break on you, especially when hand sewing! I tend to use neutral-color threads.

Cotton thread

- **Quick Press Seam Roller** (by It's Sew Emma). You're probably wondering what in the world this is. It's a quick way to press your seams down without using an iron—you literally roll them down. It sounds kind of silly, but it actually works quite well! I refer to this tool as an alternative to finger pressing; it is perfect when doing a small quilt as-you-go Log Cabin quilt in *Friday Harbor* (page 42). It can also come in handy for pressing the seams open as discussed in the QAYG assembly technique Method 1: Block-to-Block Assembly (page 95).

Quick Press Seam Roller

Photos by Estefany Gonzalez of C&T Publishing

Cutting Circles

In the *Sunset Hill* (page 32) instructions, I show you how to cut circles using a 9˝ paper plate as a guide. However, now you can find awesome rulers made specifically for cutting circles! Here are a couple that I recommend.

- **Fiskars Fabric Circle Cutter.** Fold your fabric in half and align the fold with the ruler then cut with the special push cutter to get the circle size you want.

- **Fiskars Circle Templates.** Use with Fiskars Shapexpress2 knife.

Or you can keep it real and use a paper plate! It's good to have options.

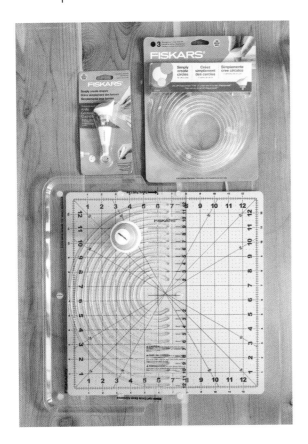

Curved Safety Pins

I totally recommend these! The curve allows the pin to pop right back up through your fabric, which will make basting a quilt so much faster and easier.

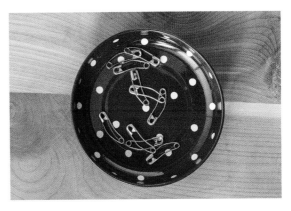

100% Wool Ironing Mat

I like this 100% wool felted ironing mat by Precision Quilting Tools because it's thick enough that you can place it on any table top. Also, it retains heat, making for a quicker press.

Photos by Estefany Gonzalez of C&T Publishing

The Best Batting for Quilt As-You-Go

NEEDLE-PUNCHED 80%+ COTTON BATTING

During any kind of quilting; whether it Is quilt as-you-go or traditional quilting, your batting will stretch or warp. It is the fluffy insulation that enables a quilt to be warm and cozy, so that is just the nature of the material! To deal with this, I buy needle-punched batting, and I cut the batting large enough to compensate for any warping.

The fibers in needle-punched batting are held together from being punched with thousands of tiny needles (as opposed to resins and glue), which creates a lower loft and dense sheet of batting that feels almost fleece-like. It is easy to work with and I have found this material to have the least amount of warping.

Photo by Estefany Gonzalez of C&T Publishing

IMPORTANT: Choose a needle-punched batting that is at least 80% cotton. Blends that have too much polyester may melt slightly if you need to press the seam open. (See the QAYG assembly technique Method 1: Block-to-Block Assembly, page 95.)

My favorites are:

- **Warm & White Batting** (by The Warm Company), 87.5% cotton / 12.5% polyester

- **Pellon 100% Cotton Batting** (with scrim, needle-punched). The Pellon Legacy line of needle-punched batting is wonderful too.

And try this precut batting:

- **Happy Cloud Silky Blend Quilt Batting** (by Fat Quarter Shop), 80% cotton and 20% polyester. I love this batting! And the best part is it comes in precut squares—8″ × 8″, 10″ × 10″, and 14″ × 14″—perfect for quilt as-you-go!

WORKING WITH BATTING

This reviews the information from my first two books, but includes good tips for starting a quilt as-you-go project.

How Large to Cut the Batting Squares

The general rule of thumb is to cut batting 1˝ bigger than the squared, or trimmed, block size. The patterns in this book will tell you exactly how big you need to cut your batting, so you won't need to worry about sizing it up. However, this is good to know if you decide to get creative and make your own size blocks.

Note: A "squared block" is the size the quilt block will be trimmed to *before* it is assembled with other blocks. This is also called the block's trim size, and is ½˝ larger than the finished size of the block.

How to Quickly Cut the Batting Squares

It may look intimidating to cut squares from a large piece of batting, but it's really simple.

You could cut it in a similar fashion as you would cut fabric squares. Using a 60mm rotary cutter allows you to cut through multiple batting layers at a time.

Or you can use a quilt block as a guide. Remember that your batting squares don't need to be cut into a perfect square; they just need to be approximately 1˝ bigger than your quilt block.

1. Place the block on the bottom corner of the batting, and use fabric scissors to cut approximately 1˝ from the edge.

2. Fold the batting upward and cut along the edge as a guide. Keep folding and cutting until you've cut a batting strip.

3. Use the block as a guide to subcut batting squares from the strip.

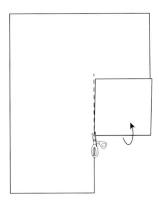

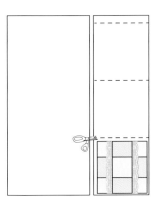

Patterns

Port Townsend
(project, page 50)

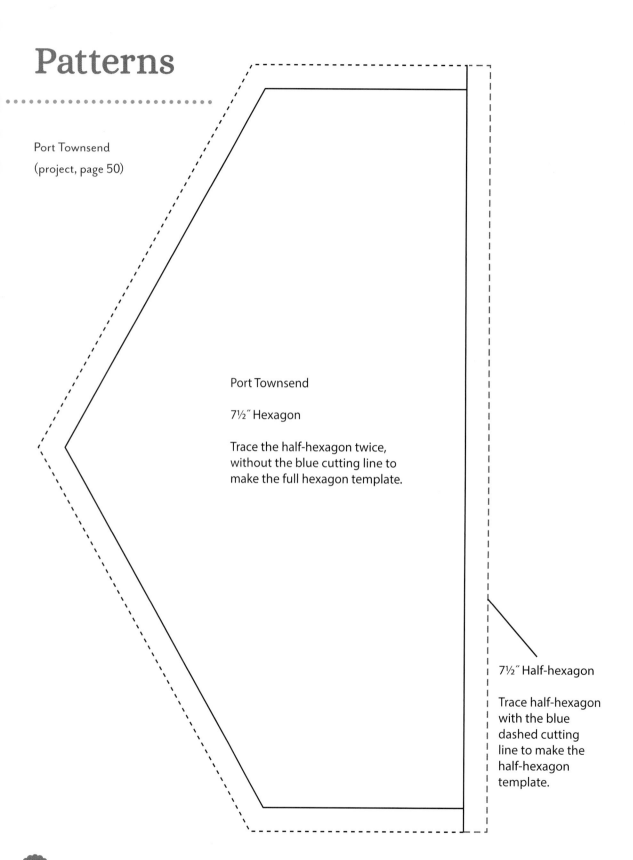

Port Townsend

7½″ Hexagon

Trace the half-hexagon twice, without the blue cutting line to make the full hexagon template.

7½″ Half-hexagon

Trace half-hexagon with the blue dashed cutting line to make the half-hexagon template.

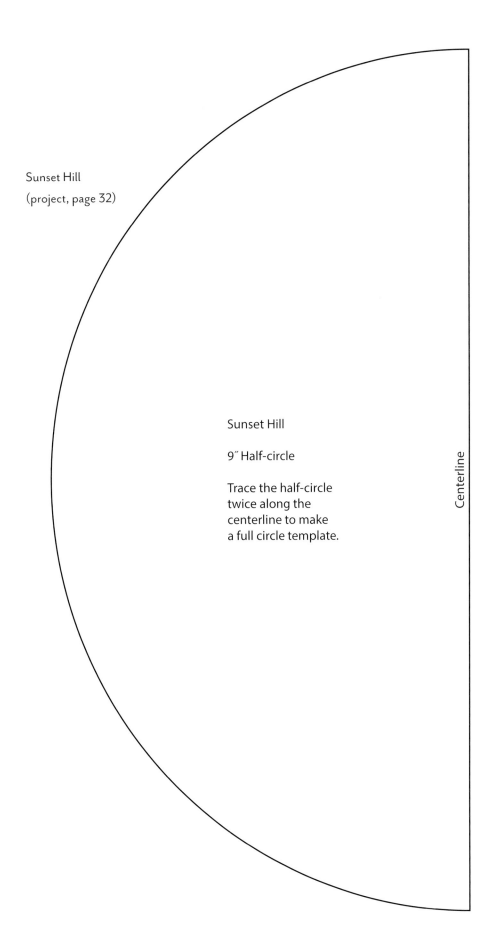

Sunset Hill
(project, page 32)

Sunset Hill

9˝ Half-circle

Trace the half-circle
twice along the
centerline to make
a full circle template.

Centerline

About the Author

Jera Brandvig (a.k.a. @QuiltingintheRain) lives in a cozy home in the rainy city of Seattle, Washington, with her two boys and wonderful husband.

After having her first son, she took a break from the biotech industry to raise her children. During that time, her creative side took over and she wrote two best-selling books, *Quilt As-You-Go Made Modern* and *Quilt As-You-Go Made Vintage*. She also designed fabric for Lecien Fabrics.

Jera has returned to biotech working full time. However, quilting will always be her true passion as she still quilts and now designs fabric for Maywood Studios.

Visit Jera online and follow on social media!

Blog: quiltingintherain.com

Facebook: /QuiltingintheRain

Instagram: @QuiltingintheRain

Also by Jera Brandvig:

 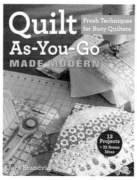

Photo by Benjamin Brandvig